MRCS System Modules: Practice Papers

Christopher LH Chan
BSc (Hons) MB BS FRCS(Eng)
Sir Alan Parks and MRC Clinical Training Fellow

Academic Department of Surgery
St Bartholomew's and the Royal London
School of Medicine and Dentistry
Whitechapel, London
and
Specialist Registrar in General Surgery
South Thames (East) Rotation

PASTEST
Dedicated to your success

© 2000 PASTEST
Egerton Court
Parkgate Estate
Knutsford
Cheshire
WA16 8DX

Telephone: 01565 752000

First published 2000

ISBN: 1 901198 46 4

A catalogue record for this book is available from the British Library.

The information contained within this book was obtained by the authors from reliable sources. However, while every effort has been made to ensure its accuracy, no responsibility for loss, damage or injury occasioned to any person acting or refraining from action as a result of information contained herein can be accepted by the publishers or authors.

PasTest Revision Books and Intensive Courses

PasTest has been established in the field of postgraduate medical education since 1972, providing revision books and intensive study courses for doctors preparing for their professional examinations. Books and courses are available for the following specialties:
MRCS, MRCP Part 1 and 2, MRCPCH Part 1 and 2, MRCPsych, MRCOG, DRCOG, MRCGP, DCH, FRCA, PLAB.

For further details contact:

PasTest, Freepost, Knutsford, Cheshire WA16 7BR
Tel: 01565 752000   Fax: 01565 650264

Text prepared by Breeze Ltd, Manchester.
Printed and bound by Ashford Colour Press, Gosport, Hants.

CONTENTS

CONTRIBUTORS

Mr Sam Andrews MA MS FRCS
Consultant General and Vascular Surgeon, Maidstone and Tunbridge Wells NHS Trust, Maidstone General Hospital, Maidstone, Kent.

Professor Martin Berry MD DSc FRCPath
Professor of Anatomy, Centre for Neuroscience, Neural Damage and Repair, Hodgkin Building, Guy's Campus, London.

Mr John Bowen FRCS (Paed)
Consultant Neonatal and Paediatric Surgeon, Department of Paediatric Surgery, Royal Manchester Children's Hospital, Pendlebury, Manchester.

Mr Christopher LH Chan Bsc(Hons) MBBS FRCS(Eng)
Sir Alan Parks and MRC Clinical Training Fellow, Academic Department of Surgery, St Bartholomew's and the Royal London School of Medicine and Dentistry, Whitechapel, London and Specialist Registrar in General Surgery, South Thames (East) Rotation.

Miss Shirley Chan FRCS
Higher Surgical Trainee, Conquest Hospital, St. Leonards on Sea, East Sussex.

Mr Matthew Dunn FRCS FFAEM DIMC DSMRSC
Consultant in Accident and Emergency, Department of Accident and Emergency, Warwick Hospital, Warwick.

Ms Deborah Eastwood MB FRCS
Consultant Orthopaedic Surgeon, (Honorary Senior Lecturer), Paediatric Unit, Royal National Orthopaedic Hospital, Brockley Hill, Stanmore, Middlesex.

Mr Jeremy J Elkabir MBBS FRCS (Eng) FRCS Urol
Senior Registrar in Urology, St George's Hospital, London.

Mr Andrew J Malouf MBBS (Syd) FRACS
Locum Consultant Colorectal Surgeon, Department of Colorectal Surgery, St Mark's Hospital, Watford Road, Harrow, London and Central Middlesex Hospital, Park Royal, London.

Dr Terry Martin MSc MB BS DRCOG DavMed MRCS DIMC RCSEd Associate Fellow FAEM
Specialist Registrar in Anaesthetics, Nuffield Department of Anaesthetics, John Radcliffe Hospital, Oxford.

Mr Charles Maxwell-Armstrong DM FRCS
Specialist Registrar in General Surgery, Department of Surgery, Queen's Medical Centre, Nottingham.

Mr John Mosley BSc MD MRCP FRCS (England and Edinburgh)
Consultant General Surgeon, Leigh Infirmary, Leigh, Lancashire.

Dr Andrew Mumford BSc MB ChB MRCP
Research Fellow, MRC Haemostasis Research Group, Clinical Sciences Centre, Hammersmith Hospital, London.

Dr R E Shanthakumar MB BS FFARCSI FRCA EDICM
Consultant Anaesthetist, Department of Anaesthetics, Barnet General Hospital, Barnet, Herts.

Dr David Southern FRCA
Consultant Anaesthetist, Department of Anaesthesia, Wrexham Maelor Hospital, Wrexham, North Wales.

PREFACE

This book is intended primarily for candidates sitting the System MCQ section of the MRCS/AFRCS examination. The papers have been specifically structured as Practice papers and aim to reflect the Royal College Syllabus.

The goal of such a book is to provide an adjunct to reading, help assess knowledge and alert one to areas that require further study. In addition, this book has covered the favourite topics that appear in the MRCS/AFRCS examinations. MCQ practice will increase basic knowledge and detailed explanations have been written to aid revision. The explanations should also be useful to candidates in other parts of the examination.

I hope that this book will not be restricted only to candidates sitting the MRCS/AFRCS examination but will also be of use to Final Year medical students.

Christopher Chan
August 2000

INTRODUCTION

In 1997 the structure of the surgical professional examinations underwent a series of major changes, in which the old-style FRCS exam was replaced by the new 'entry-level' qualifications of the MRCS (MRCSEd, MRCS (Glasg.) or AFRCSI). A pass is required in all sections of the MRCS Diploma Examination, which is taken during approved basic surgical training (24 month period). Having completed the MRCS, the trainee can then apply for a national training number (NTN) and commence higher surgical training in his or her chosen surgical specialty. A final exit examination is then required in that specialty. A pass in the Intercollegiate specialty examination awards the candidate with the 'full' Fellowship of the Royal College of Surgeons (FRCS). Providing training has been adequately completed, the trainee can then apply for a certificate of completion of Surgical Training (CCST) and be placed on the GMC register and so be eligible to apply for a consultant post.

Membership of the Royal College of Surgeons of England (MRCS) examination consists of three sections:

1. Two multiple choice papers: (conducted twice a year)
   Paper 1 – Core Modules (2 hrs duration)
   Paper 2 – System Modules (2 hrs duration)
2. A Clinical Section (conducted twice a year)
3. A Viva Voce section (conducted twice a year)

The first section consists of two multiple choice papers. Paper 1 Core Modules tests knowledge of peri-operative management, trauma, intensive care, neoplasia, techniques and outcomes of surgery. Paper 2 System Modules involves specific systems: locomotor, vascular, abdominal, head, neck, endocrine and paediatric, urology and transplantation. These subjects are tested using a combination of multiple choice questions and extended matching questions. Candidates may sit each of the MCQ papers as often as they wish. There is full reciprocity of recognition of a 'pass' in the whole MCQ section between all three UK Royal Surgical Colleges and the Royal College of Surgeons of Ireland.

The candidate then progresses to the Clinical and Viva sections of the exam. For the London MRCS exam a candidate must pass the written papers before sitting the clinical examination, and pass both written and clinical before being invited to the Viva. In other colleges the order varies slightly. Only when a candidate has passed all three parts are they awarded the MRCS Diploma.

MCQ EXAMINATION TECHNIQUE

Exam technique

Before sitting an MCQ examination, you will need to know how many questions are likely to be on the paper and how long you will be given to complete it. Thus you will be able to assess the approximate amount of time that can be spent on each question. The time allotted for each of the written papers is **two hours**. Different questions are used each time, therefore subject composition is variable from exam to exam. There are approximately 45 MCQs and around 20 EMQs, depending upon the number of responses required.

Pacing yourself accurately during the examination to finish on time, or with time to spare, is essential. You must also decide on your own personal strategy for approaching the paper. You may decide to read quickly through the paper before picking up your pen, or to work slowly through the paper answering everything that you are certain of and leaving anything you wish to come back to.

There are two common mistakes which cause good candidates to fail the MRCS written examinations. These are neglecting to read the directions and questions carefully enough and failing to fill in the computer answer card properly. You must read the instructions to candidates at the beginning of each section of the paper to ensure that you complete the answer sheet correctly. You must also ensure that you read the question (both stem and items) carefully. Regard each item as being independent of every other item, each referring to a specific quantum of knowledge. The item (or the stem and the item taken together) make up a statement as 'True' or 'False'. The number of stems will vary for each question. For this reason, a mark will not necessarily be required for each column of the answer sheet. For every correct answer you will gain a mark (+1). For the MRCS (London) examination, marks will not be deducted for a wrong answer. Equally, you will not gain a mark if you mark both true and false.

You must also decide on a strategy to follow with regard to marking your answers. The answer sheet is read by an automatic document reader, which transfers the information it reads to a computer. It is critical that the answer sheet is filled in clearly and accurately using the pencils provided. Failure to fill in your name and your examination correctly could result in the rejection of your paper. Some candidates mark their answers directly onto the computer sheet as they go through the question, others prefer to make a note of their answers on the question paper, and reserve time at the end to transfer their answers onto the computer sheet. If you choose the first method, there is a chance that you may decide to change your answer after a second reading. If you do change your answer on the computer sheet, you must ensure that your original is thoroughly erased. If you choose the second method, make sure that you allow enough time to transfer your answers methodically onto the computer sheet, as rushing at this stage could introduce some costly mistakes. You will find it less confusing if you transfer your marks after you have completed each section of the examination. You must ensure that you have left sufficient time to transfer your marks from the question paper to the answer sheet. You should also be aware that no additional time will be given at the end of the examination to allow you to transfer your marks.

If you find that you have time left at the end of the examination, there can be a temptation to re-read your answers time and time again, so that even those that seemed straightforward will start to look less convincing. In this situation, first thoughts are usually the best, don't alter your initial answers unless you are sure. Don't be afraid to leave the examination room once you are satisfied with your answers.

To guess or not to guess

Tests carried out at PasTest's MRCS intensive revision courses have proved that most candidates can improve their marks by making sensible guesses.

The MRCS exams in England are not negatively marked[1]. For this reason you should answer every question as you have nothing to lose. If you do not know the answer to a question, you should make an educated guess – you may well get the answer right and gain a mark.

If you feel that you need to spend more time puzzling over a question, leave it and, if you have time, return to it. Make sure you have collected all the marks you can before you come back to any difficult questions.

Final advice

Multiple choice questions are not designed to trick you or confuse you, they are designed to test your knowledge of medicine. Accept each question at its face value, do not look for hidden meanings or catches. The aim of this book is to enable you to evaluate your level of knowledge by working through the questions in each section. By marking clearly all of the answers that you got wrong or declined to answer, you can then refresh your memory with the explanations given here or read up on specific topics in depth using a textbook.

Working through the questions in this book will help you to identify your weak subject areas. Using books and lectures, you must work out your own personal profile of strengths and weaknesses and plan your revision accordingly. In the last few weeks before the exam it will be important for you to avoid minor unimportant areas and concentrate on the most important subject areas covered in the exam.

---

[1] The AFRCS examinations in Scotland are currently negatively marked.

SAMPLE MCQ ANSWER SHEET

Sample answer sheet, reproduced by kind permission of
the Royal College of Surgeons of England

SAMPLE EMQ ANSWER SHEET

Each question will have up to ten options listed (A–J). Only one of the options will be the correct answer. Indicate your response by marking a single line through the appropriate box.

For example:

Question 61 correct answer is option C
Question 62 correct answer is option F
Question 63 correct answer is option A

Sample answer sheet, reproduced by kind permission of
the Royal College of Surgeons of England

GLOSSARY

5-FU	5-fluorouracil
AAA	Abdominal aortic aneurysms
ACTH	Adrenocorticotropic hormone
ADH	Anti-diuretic hormone
ANOVA	Analysis of variance
ANP	Atrial natriuretic peptide
AP	Antero-posterior
APTT	Activated partial thromboplastin time
ARDS	Adult respiratory distress syndrome
ARF	Acute renal failure
AXR	Abdominal X-ray
BCC	Basal cell carcinoma
BPH	Benign prostatic hyperplasia
CEA	Carcinoembryonic antigen
CPAP	Continuous positive airway pressure
CPP	Central perfusion pressure
CPR	Cardio pulmonary resuscitation
CRP	cAMP receptor protein, C-reactive protein
CSF	Cerebro spinal fluid
CT	Computerised tomography
CVP	Central venous pressure
CXR	Chest X-ray
DCIS	Ductal carcinoma in situ
DES	Diethylstilbestrol
DIC	Disseminated intravascular coagulation
DMSA scan	Dimercaptosuccinic acid
DPL	Diagnostic peritoneal lavage
DTPA scan	Diethylene triamine penta-acetic
ECG	Electrocardiograph
ERC	European resuscitation council
ERCP	Endoscopic retrograde cholangiopancreatography
ESR	Erythrocyte sedimentation rate
ESWL	Extra-corporeal shock wave lithotripsy
EUA	Examination under anaesthetic
FAP	Familial adenomatous polyposis
FBC	Full blood count
FFAs	Free fatty acids
FFP	Fresh frozen plasma
FIB	Fibrinogen
FNAC	Fine needle aspiration cytology
FOBT	Faecal occult blood testing
FRC	Functional residual capacity
GCS	Glasgow Coma Scale

GFR	Glomerular filtration rate
GI	Gastrointestinal
GTN	Glyceryl trinitrate
GVHD	Graft versus host disease
HIFU	High intensity focused ultrasound
HNPCC	Hereditary non-polyposis colorectal cancer
IBD	Inflammatory bowel disease
ICP	Intracranial pressure
IDDM	Insulin dependent diabetes mellitus
INR	International normalised ratio
ITGCN	Intra-tubular germ cell neoplasia
IVU	Intravenous urogram
KUB	Kidneys, ureter, bladder
LMWH	Low molecular weight heparins
MAOIs	Monoamine oxidase inhibitors
MAP	Mean arterial blood pressure
MEN	Multiple endocrine neoplasia
MIBG scan	Meta-iodobenzyl guanidine
MODS	Multiple organ dysfunction syndrome
MRA	Magnetic resonance angiography
MRSA	Methicillin-resistant Staphylococcus aureus
MSU	Midstream urine
NEC	Necrotizing enterocolitis
NSAID	Non-steroidal anti-inflammatory drugs
OA	Oesophageal atresia
PCNL	Percutaneous nephrolithotomy
PEEP	Positive end expiratory pressure
PMC	Pseudomembranous colitis
PSA	Prostatic specific antigen
PT	Prothrombin time
PUJ	Pelvi-ureteric junction
RBC	Red blood cells
RCC	Renal cell carcinoma
RTA	Road traffic accident
SCC	Squamous cell carcinoma
SSG	Split skin grafting
TIA	Transient ischaemic attack
TOF	Tracheo-oesophageal fistula
TPN	Total parenteral nutrition
TRUS	Transrectal ultrasound scan
TT	Thrombin time
TURBT	Trans-urethral resection
TURP	Transurethral resection of the prostate
UDT	Undescended testis
UTI	Urinary Tract Infection
vWF	von Willebrand factor
WBC	White blood cells

Time allowed: 2 hours
Indicate your answers in the spaces provided

SYSTEM PAPER 1
SECTION 1 – MCQS

1. **Invasive follicular carcinoma of the thyroid**

   ❑ A   is usually multifocal
   ❑ B   commonly spreads to lymph nodes
   ❑ C   may be accurately differentiated from follicular adenoma by fine needle aspiration cytology
   ❑ D   should be treated by total thyroidectomy
   ❑ E   has a better prognosis in children

2. **Papillary carcinoma of the thyroid**

   ❑ A   has an equal sex incidence
   ❑ B   has a median age of onset in the fourth decade
   ❑ C   arises from stromal cells
   ❑ D   is associated with low-iodine intake
   ❑ E   may form part of Multiple Endocrine Neoplasia Type I

3. **Salivary gland calculi**

   ❑ A   usually arise in the parotid gland
   ❑ B   are most commonly found in the sixth decade
   ❑ C   are associated with a more alkaline saliva
   ❑ D   are more common in diabetics
   ❑ E   are mostly visible on plain X-ray

4. **Midline swellings of the neck include**

   ❑ A   cystic hygromas
   ❑ B   plunging ranulas
   ❑ C   subhyoid bursas
   ❑ D   branchial cysts
   ❑ E   arteriovenous fistulae

5.   The parotid gland

❑ A   is encapsulated by the investing layer of deep cervical fascia
❑ B   receives its blood supply directly from the external carotid
        artery
❑ C   is traversed by the facial artery
❑ D   is separated from the carotid sheath by the styloid process
❑ E   contains the common facial vein

6.   Application of arterial clips during total thyroidectomy could injure the following nerves:

❑ A   recurrent laryngeal
❑ B   internal laryngeal
❑ C   external laryngeal
❑ D   phrenic
❑ E   transverse cervical

7.   Resection of the terminal ileum is associated with malabsorption of

❑ A   calcium
❑ B   vitamin B_{12}
❑ C   folic acid
❑ D   cholesterol
❑ E   bile salts

8.   The following may be seen in the blood film of a post-splenectomy patient:

❑ A   target cells
❑ B   punctate basophilia
❑ C   Howell-Jolly bodies
❑ D   sideroblasts
❑ E   rouleaux formation

9.   **Squamous cell carcinoma of the anal canal**

- ❏ A   may spread to pelvic lymph nodes
- ❏ B   is associated with human papilloma virus infection
- ❏ C   characteristically presents with faecal incontinence
- ❏ D   is relatively radio-resistant
- ❏ E   is related to increased dietary fat intake

10.   **Regarding patients with jaundice**

- ❏ A   urobilinogen in the urine suggests a post-hepatic cause
- ❏ B   bilirubin in the urine suggests a pre-hepatic cause
- ❏ C   a markedly elevated serum alkaline phosphatase is an indicator of post-hepatic disease
- ❏ D   a raised serum gamma glutamyl transferase is an indicator of a pre-hepatic cause
- ❏ E   dark urine and pale stools are indicators of a post-hepatic cause

11.   **Indications for ERCP include**

- ❏ A   cholelithiasis
- ❏ B   pancreatic pseudocyst
- ❏ C   empyema of the gall bladder
- ❏ D   ascending cholangitis
- ❏ E   pancreatic divisum

12.   **Extra-intestinal manifestations of Gardner's syndrome include**

- ❏ A   osteomas
- ❏ B   erythema marginatum
- ❏ C   multinodular goitre
- ❏ D   epidermoid cysts
- ❏ E   tenosynovitis

13.   Regarding choledocholithiasis

❑   A   approximately 15% of patients with acute cholecystitis will have CBD stones
❑   B   CBD stones of 10 mm or less will usually pass spontaneously into the duodenum without complication
❑   C   intra-operative cholangiography misses CBD stones in 25% of cases
❑   D   ERCP stone extraction can usually be achieved without sphincterotomy
❑   E   liver function tests deteriorate before they improve following surgical removal of stones

14.   Meckel's diverticulum

❑   A   may be seen on HIDA scan
❑   B   occurs in approximately 8% of people
❑   C   usually occurs in the proximal jejunum
❑   D   may contain ectopic adrenal tissue
❑   E   usually presents with complications

15.   Concerning pseudomembranous colitis

❑   A   it may occur following the use of cefuroxime
❑   B   *Clostridium difficile* is a normal commensal of the gut
❑   C   *Clostridium difficile* toxin can be isolated in the stool of over 90% of affected patients
❑   D   it typically produces grey nodules on the mucosal surface
❑   E   it may progress to toxic megacolon
❑   F   the treatment of choice is oral erythromycin

16.   Extra-intestinal manifestations of inflammatory bowel disease (IBD) include

❑   A   exophthalmos
❑   B   abnormalities of liver function tests
❑   C   primary sclerosing cholangitis
❑   D   hepatic adenoma
❑   E   ankylosing spondylitis
❑   F   urinary calculi formation

4

17.   Regarding Crohn's disease

❑   A   smoking confers protection
❑   B   smoking does not alter the risk of post-operative recurrence
             after surgery
❑   C   viruses have been shown to have a definite causal relationship
❑   D   25% of patients have a positive family history
❑   E   the risk of a child of an affected patient developing Crohn's
             disease is approximately 25%

18.   In cases of severe ulcerative colitis

❑   A   abdominal signs are unaltered by steroids
❑   B   the ESR is elevated but the CRP remains normal
❑   C   sequential plain AXRs are an important means of patient
             monitoring
❑   D   any patient with a colonic diameter of > 6.5 cm has toxic
             megacolon
❑   E   growth retardation may be a feature in children

19.   Entero-vesical fistulae

❑   A   are secondary to diverticular disease in approximately 50% of
             cases
❑   B   present with pneumaturia in over 50% of cases
❑   C   lead to faecaluria in 75% of cases
❑   D   are secondary to colorectal cancer in approximately 50%
             cases
❑   E   rarely complicate Crohn's disease

20.   Pancreatic carcinoma

❑   A   rarely develops before the fifth decade
❑   B   is more common in men
❑   C   is associated with smoking
❑   D   responds well to 5 FU treatment
❑   E   frequently presents with a palpable gall bladder

21. Abdominal aortic aneurysm

- ❑ A may cause embolization to lower limbs
- ❑ B is more common in males
- ❑ C can almost always be treated by endovascular stenting
- ❑ D can be detected by screening
- ❑ E should be operated upon when it is 5.5 cm long

22. Regarding vascular lesions of the skin

- ❑ A naevus flammeus (salmon patch) is the common birthmark
- ❑ B port wine stains show little tendency to regress with time
- ❑ C spider naevi are venular in origin
- ❑ D juvenile haemangiomas usually involute by the age of 7 years
- ❑ E cavernous haemangiomas usually involute with time

23. Critical leg ischaemia

- ❑ A is defined as persistently recurring rest pain requiring adequate analgesia for more than two months with an ankle systolic pressure of < 50 mmHg and/or a toe systolic pressure of < 30 mmHg
- ❑ B is defined as ulceration or gangrene of foot or toes with an ankle systolic pressure of < 50 mmHg and/or a toe pressure of < 30 mmHg
- ❑ C is defined as persistently recurring rest pain requiring adequate analgesia for more than one week, with associated ulceration or gangrene of the foot and toes, with an ankle systolic pressure of < 70 mmHg and/or a toe pressure of < 40 mmHg
- ❑ D can be treated by intra-arterial thrombolysis
- ❑ E with digital gangrene can be effectively treated with lumbar sympathectomy

24. The external inguinal ring

- ❑ A is formed by a V-shaped slit in the internal oblique aponeurosis
- ❑ B transmits the testicular artery
- ❑ C transmits the cremasteric artery
- ❑ D transmits the femoral branch of the genito-femoral nerve
- ❑ E transmits the pampiniform plexus
- ❑ F transmits the iliohypogastric nerve
- ❑ G transmits the cremasteric muscle

25. In the anatomy of the femoral region the

- ❑ A femoral sheath contains the femoral vessels
- ❑ B femoral canal lies lateral to the femoral vein
- ❑ C femoral canal contains Cloquet's lymph node
- ❑ D femoral ring is the abdominal end of the femoral canal
- ❑ E pubic branch of the inferior epigastric vein replaces the obturator vein in 30% of cases

26. Within the orbit

- ❑ A the optic nerve is invested by meninges
- ❑ B ischaemic necrosis of the retina follows optic nerve crush/ transection
- ❑ C blow-out fractures can cause diplopia
- ❑ D trochlear nerve lesions cause ptosis
- ❑ E frontal nerve lesions depress the corneal reflex

27. The brachial artery is

- ❑ A palpable in the arm
- ❑ B crossed anteriorly by the median nerve
- ❑ C overlain by the biceps tendon
- ❑ D surrounded by a venae comitantes
- ❑ E accompanied by the ulnar nerve

28. **The carpal tunnel contains the**

- ❑ A median nerve
- ❑ B ulnar nerve
- ❑ C ulnar artery
- ❑ D flexor carpi ulnaris tendon
- ❑ E flexor carpi radialis tendon

29. **The greater sciatic foramen contains the**

- ❑ A superior gluteal nerve
- ❑ B sacrospinous ligament as a boundary
- ❑ C pudendal nerve
- ❑ D obturator internus tendon
- ❑ E posterior femoral cutaneous nerve

30. **In the femoral triangle the**

- ❑ A cribriform fascia transmits the superficial branches of the femoral artery
- ❑ B femoral vein lies adjacent to the femoral nerve
- ❑ C profunda femoris artery lies medial to the femoral artery
- ❑ D femoral sheath extends some 3 cm beyond the inguinal ligament
- ❑ E deep inguinal nodes lie medial to the femoral vein

31. **A typical thoracic vertebra**

- ❑ A articulates with four ribs
- ❑ B allows flexion and extension of the trunk
- ❑ C has a basivertebral foramen
- ❑ D has an articular facet on each transverse process
- ❑ E has intervertebral cartilaginous joints

32.   **The appendix normally**

☐   A   arises from the antero-inferior aspect of the caecum
☐   B   lies medial to the right ureter
☐   C   has taeniae coli
☐   D   lies on the right gonadal vessels
☐   E   has an avascular mesoappendix

33.   **The left ureter lies**

☐   A   anterior to the left gonadal vessels
☐   B   posterior to the left colic artery
☐   C   anterior to the genito-femoral nerve
☐   D   in the apex of the sigmoid mesocolon
☐   E   anterior (above) the left ductus (vas) deferens

34.   **The spleen**

☐   A   is related to the left costodiaphragmatic recess
☐   B   lies against the pancreas
☐   C   must double in size to be palpable
☐   D   is attached to the stomach by the lienorenal ligament
☐   E   has the lesser sac extending into the hilum

35.   **In the female reproductive tract**

☐   A   the ovarian artery supplies the Fallopian tube
☐   B   most of the anterior surface of the uterus is covered by peritoneum
☐   C   ureteric calculi are palpable per vaginum
☐   D   the ovary lies posterior to the broad ligament
☐   E   lymph drains from the uterine tubes to the superficial inguinal lymph nodes

36. **The rectum**

☐ A has a venous drainage via the portal vein
☐ B has a mesentery
☐ C has its lower third covered by peritoneum
☐ D lies against the vagina
☐ E has a lymphatic drainage via the inguinal lymph nodes

37. **The anal canal**

☐ A lies below the levator ani muscle
☐ B has a longitudinal muscular coat
☐ C has a lymphatic drainage via the inguinal lymph nodes
☐ D has an external sphincter innervated by the pudendal nerve
☐ E possesses valves

38. **Common indications for considering internal fixation of fractures include**

☐ A pathological fractures
☐ B intra-articular fractures
☐ C open fractures
☐ D post open exploration of a concomitant vascular injury
☐ E failure to achieve a closed reduction of a simple closed fracture

39. **Management of a compound fracture of the proximal femur includes**

☐ A application of a plaster cast
☐ B anti-tetanus toxoid
☐ C oral antibiotics
☐ D iodine dressing to wound
☐ E assessment of the Glasgow Coma Scale (GCS)

40. **Testicular torsion**

☐ A is associated with Henoch-Schönlein purpura
☐ B is more commonly found in men with a history of mal-descended testes
☐ C can be reliably diagnosed by ultrasound
☐ D may be imitated by torsion of the hydatid of Morgagni
☐ E may be associated with UTIs

41. **Congenital hypertrophic pyloric stenosis**

☐ A typically presents at birth
☐ B is more common in males
☐ C may result in hypocalcaemia
☐ D may result in a metabolic alkalosis
☐ E is best investigated by contrast examination

42. **Abdominal pain in a 4-year-old girl can be the presenting feature of**

☐ A pneumonia
☐ B intussusception
☐ C meningitis
☐ D viral infection
☐ E intestinal atresia

43. **Hirschsprung's disease**

☐ A almost always involves the rectum
☐ B can involve the entire intestine
☐ C is continuous in its distribution
☐ D is characterised by an excess of ganglion cells in the myenteric plexus
☐ E may present in adulthood

44. **A term infant, weighing 3.1 kg**

- [ ] A   requires about 450 ml of formula milk daily for adequate fluid and calories
- [ ] B   should be maintained on 700 ml of normal saline per day intravenously
- [ ] C   is at high risk of necrotizing enterocolitis (NEC)
- [ ] D   is at risk of developing hypoglycaemia post-operatively
- [ ] E   should pass meconium in the first 24 hours after birth

45. **Carcinoma of the prostate**

- [ ] A   is the commonest adult male tumour in the UK
- [ ] B   occurs in > 30% of men over 50 years
- [ ] C   70% of tumours arise in the peripheral zone
- [ ] D   is more common in Caucasians
- [ ] E   has a 3 times increased risk if two first-degree relatives are affected

46. **Renal cell carcinoma**

- [ ] A   is associated with von Recklinghausen's disease
- [ ] B   is usually detected incidentally on ultrasound examination
- [ ] C   most commonly presents with loin pain
- [ ] D   tumours < 4 cm at either pole should be treated by partial nephrectomy if possible
- [ ] E   is multifocal in over 40% of cases

47. **A 77-year-old male presents with lower urinary tract symptoms. A digital rectal examination shows a hard irregular mass which appears to extend outside the normal prostate. The following investigation(s)/treatment(s) are indicated:**

- [ ] A   PSA
- [ ] B   TURP sending all tissue for histology
- [ ] C   TRUS and biopsies
- [ ] D   pelvic X-ray
- [ ] E   bone scan
- [ ] F   immediate treatment with diethylstilboestrol (DES) and aspirin

48. **The following stones are radiolucent:**

- [ ] A calcium oxalate
- [ ] B staghorn calculi
- [ ] C urate calculi
- [ ] D cysteine calculi
- [ ] E xanthine calculi

49. **Absolute indications for TURP include**

- [ ] A obstructive uropathy with renal impairment
- [ ] B bladder calculus
- [ ] C recurrent prostatitis
- [ ] D persistent haematuria of prostatic origin
- [ ] E residual volume of > 200 ml

50. **The following statements concerning prostatitis are true:**

- [ ] A chronic abacterial prostatitis is associated with an absence of white cells on expressed prostatic secretions
- [ ] B acute bacterial prostatitis may require TURP
- [ ] C all relevant investigations in prostatodynia are negative
- [ ] D chronic bacterial prostatitis is treated with a one week course of antibiotics
- [ ] E younger patients (i.e. < 35 years) with chronic abacterial prostatitis should always be treated with doxycycline

51. **Concerning renal transplantation**

- [ ] A the donor kidney is usually sited in an intraperitoneal position
- [ ] B transplantation of a left donor kidney is more technically demanding
- [ ] C a large post-operative lymphocele is treated with peritoneal windowing
- [ ] D graft survival following living donor transplant is equivalent to cadaveric transplants
- [ ] E patients with a history of treated primary brain tumour are suitable donors

52. **Regular (1–2 yearly) colonoscopic surveillance for ulcerative colitis is indicated for**

❏ A patients with early onset of disease regardless of extent or duration of disease

❏ B patients with long-standing disease proximal to the splenic flexure

❏ C patients with extraintestinal manifestations of ulcerative colitis regardless of the extent and duration of disease

❏ D patients with confirmed high grade dysplasia identified on previous colonic biopsies

SECTION 2 – EMQs

Theme: Investigation of carotid artery disease

A   Duplex Doppler ultrasound of carotid arteries
B   Carotid angiography
C   CT scan of head
D   Magnetic Resonance Angiography (MRA)
E   Transcranial Doppler ultrasound
F   Near infra-red spectroscopy

From each of the statements below, select the most appropriate investigation from the list above. Each option may be used once, more than once or not at all.

☐   61.   The first-line (initial) investigation in a 65-year-old man presenting with an episode of amaurosis fugax affecting his right eye

☐   62.   A 28-year-old girl collapses with a possible dense, right-sided stroke

☐   63.   For intra-operative monitoring during carotid endarterectomy

Theme: Leg ulcers

A   Arterial
B   Venous
C   Diabetic
D   Post-phlebitic
E   Neoplastic

For each of the patient scenarios below, select the aetiology of the most likely ulcer from the list above. Each option may be used once, more than once or not at all.

☐ 64. A 72-year-old lady presents with a two year history of an intermittently healing, shallow ulcer above the right medial malleolus. The surrounding skin has a brown discoloration. Ten years previously, she was involved in a RTA and sustained pelvic fractures, treated with traction and bed rest.

☐ 65. A 68-year-old man presents with a deep, painless ulcer beneath the heel of his right foot, which has gradually deteriorated in the two months since his admission for pneumonia. The ulcer is surrounded by wet macerated skin and culture has grown MRSA and pseudomonas.

☐ 66. A 94-year-old man presents with a deep, painful ulcer at the tip of his great toe. He has gradually been getting less mobile over the last few months and the pain in his toe stops him from sleeping.

Theme: Types of ulceration

A   Curling's ulcer
B   Cushing's ulcer
C   Marjolin's ulcer
D   Stress ulcers
E   Pyoderma gangrenosum

For each of the clinical scenarios listed below, select the lesion most likely to occur in that scenario from the list above. Each option may be used once, more than once, or not at all.

☐ 67. Squamous cell carcinoma in a chronic venous ulcer
☐ 68. Head injury
☐ 69. Major burns
☐ 70. Major thoraco-abdominal trauma
☐ 71. Inflammatory bowel disease

Theme: Surgical investigations

A   Gastrografin enema
B   Abdominal CT scan
C   Small bowel follow-through
D   ERCP
E   Abdominal and pelvic ultrasound
F   Barium enema (double contrast)
G   Colonoscopy

For each of the following scenarios, select the most appropriate investigation from the list above. Each option may be used once, more than once, or not at all.

72. Hepatic hydatid cyst
73. Uncomplicated diverticular disease of the colon
74. Sclerosing cholangitis
75. Choledocholithiasis
76. Psoas abscess
77. Small bowel tumour
78. Colovesical fistula
79. Pancreatic necrosis

Theme: Anatomy of the viscera and organs in the abdomen

A   Supra-renal gland
B   Ileum
C   Coronary ligament
D   Stomach
E   Spleen
F   Pancreas
G   Meckel's diverticulum
H   Kidney

For each of the statements below, select the most likely option from the list above. Each option may be used once, more than once or not at all.

80. Is crossed by the inferior mesenteric vein
81. Has a mesentery attached to the pelvic brim
82. Has a venous drainage into the inferior vena cava
83. Has an umbilical attachment
84. Lies in the lienorenal ligament
85. Has veins forming portosystemic anastomoses

Theme: Low back pain

A Prolapsed intervertebral disc
B Muscle strain
C Facet joint arthrosis
D Osteoporotic collapse
E Metastatic disease
F Spondylolisthesis
G Discitis

For each of the clinical situations described below, please select the most likely diagnosis from the list above. Each option may be used once, more than once or not at all.

❑ 86. A teenage boy presents to his GP with a six month history of increasing pain and stiffness in the lower lumbar spine. There is no history of trauma although he is an active sportsman. His lumbar spine is stiff to examination and there is bilateral limitation of straight leg raise with pain in the hamstring muscles.

❑ 87. A young man wakes up one morning complaining of pain in his lower back. The day before he had been redecorating his daughter's bedroom. There are no nerve root signs but his back is very stiff.

❑ 88. A sprightly 88-year-old lady has had some back pain since she stumbled over her own door step six weeks ago. Her back was initially stiff but she feels there has been some improvement over the last two weeks.

❑ 89. A baby girl aged three refuses to walk. Her symptoms began last night and she is irritable and unwell. Examination of her lower limbs is entirely normal but percussion of her lumbar spine causes her to cry.

❑ 90. A 45-year-old man gives a three month history of low back pain which has become progressively worse such that he is now in agony and cannot get comfortable. The pain radiates to both buttocks and neurological examination suggests that there are problems with the sacral nerve roots.

Theme: Transitional cell carcinoma

A   TURBT
B   Intravesical mitomycin
C   Intravesical BCG
D   M-VAC chemotherapy
E   Radical cystectomy
F   Nephrectomy
G   Nephroureterectomy
H   Cystoscopy

For each of the patients below, select the most appropriate treatment from the list above. Each option may be used once, more than once or not at all.

☐ 91. A 64-year-old male presents with haematuria. An IVU shows normal upper tracts with a filling defect in the bladder. Flexible cystoscopy confirms a tumour.

☐ 92. A 58-year-old female with a history of superficial bladder cancer is found to have an irregular filling defect in the right renal pelvis. CT confirms a solid mass.

☐ 93. A fit 55-year-old male presents with haematuria. Investigations reveal a bladder tumour. A TURBT shows a muscle-invasive bladder cancer (stage T2) and EUA confirms the bladder is mobile. CT scanning shows three 2–3 cm pelvic lymph nodes.

Theme: Neonatal surgical diagnoses

A   Hirschsprung's disease
B   Oesophageal atresia
C   Tracheo-oesophageal fistula
D   Imperforate anus
E   Duodenal atresia
F   Gastroschisis
G   Exomphalos
H   Midgut volvulus
I   Necrotizing enterocolitis (NEC)

For each of the clinical scenarios given below, select the most likely diagnosis from the list above. Each option may be used once, more than once or not at all.

❑   94.   A male infant with Trisomy 21, born at term, presenting with abdominal distension, bile stained vomiting and collapse
❑   95.   An ante-natal observation of intestine and liver outside the foetal abdomen
❑   96.   A previously well male, 6-weeks-old and born at 35 weeks gestation, presenting with bile stained vomiting
❑   97.   A 4-hour-old female, noted to be 'frothy', born to a mother with polyhydramnios during pregnancy
❑   98.   An 8-day-old female infant presenting with respiratory distress with each oral feed

END OF SYSTEM PAPER 1

Time allowed: 2 hours
Indicate your answers in the spaces provided

SYSTEM PAPER 2
SECTION 1 – MCQS

1.   Acute otitis media

❑   A   is often accompanied by a purulent discharge from the ear
❑   B   is usually caused by *E. coli*
❑   C   rarely causes constitutional upset in children
❑   D   invariably forms a cholesteatoma if resolution does not occur
            by six weeks
❑   E   is primarily treated with myringotomy

2.   Oral cavity cancer

❑   A   has no sex predilection
❑   B   is most commonly found on the anterior two-thirds of the
            tongue
❑   C   rarely presents with pain
❑   D   responds well to chemotherapy
❑   E   should be treated with surgery if bony invasion occurs

3.   Insulin

❑   A   inhibits gluconeogenesis
❑   B   increases protein synthesis
❑   C   inhibits potassium entry into cells
❑   D   is synthesised by C cells of the pancreas
❑   E   increases glucose uptake by the brain

4.   Fat embolism

❑   A   is associated with diabetes
❑   B   only follows lower limb fractures
❑   C   produces fat in the urine
❑   D   does not occur in compound fractures
❑   E   produces petechial brain haemorrhages

5. **Charcot's triad includes**

- ☐ A abdominal tenderness
- ☐ B tachycardia
- ☐ C abdominal pain
- ☐ D jaundice
- ☐ E fever

6. **Perforated duodenal ulcer**

- ☐ A is normally situated posteriorly
- ☐ B can be treated conservatively with antibiotics
- ☐ C is usually found in the second part of the duodenum
- ☐ D may be repaired by an omental patch
- ☐ E may be treated by a partial gastrectomy

7. **Primary peritonitis**

- ☐ A is usually caused by haematogenous spread of a single type of bacterium
- ☐ B has a strong association with cirrhosis of the liver
- ☐ C is associated with an ascitic eosinophilia
- ☐ D has a strong association with nephrosis
- ☐ E is most commonly caused by a Gram-positive coccus

8. **Pancreatic carcinoma**

- ☐ A 40% of cases arise in the neck of the pancreas
- ☐ B is better visualised by CT than by ultrasound
- ☐ C produces typical radiological features on ERCP
- ☐ D CT features suggestive of irresectability include a portal vein of < 8 mm

9. **The following may be seen in a patient three months post-gastrectomy:**

❏ A   hypoglycaemia (early dumping syndrome)
❏ B   macrocytic anaemia
❏ C   bilious vomiting
❏ D   iron deficiency anaemia
❏ E   afferent loop syndrome

10. **Hepatobiliary complications of Crohn's disease include**

❏ A   cirrhosis
❏ B   cholangiocarcinoma
❏ C   pyoderma gangrenosum
❏ D   amyloid deposition
❏ E   haemochromatosis

11. **Radiological features of Crohn's disease on barium follow through include**

❏ A   thinning of the valvulae conniventes
❏ B   fistulae to other intraperitoneal viscera
❏ C   rose thorn ulcers
❏ D   intra-mural cysts
❏ E   thinning of the bowel wall

12. **Typical endoscopic features of ulcerative colitis include**

❏ A   mucosal granularity
❏ B   pseudopolyps
❏ C   microadenomas
❏ D   contact bleeding
❏ E   cobblestone ulceration

13. **Associated features of familial adenomatous polyposis (FAP) include**

☐ A   atrophic gastritis
☐ B   gastric adenomas
☐ C   duodenal adenomas
☐ D   uveitis
☐ E   medullary thyroid cancer

14. **Carcinoid tumours**

☐ A   are most commonly found in the large bowel
☐ B   of the small bowel are most frequently found in the ileum
☐ C   of the large bowel are most frequently found in the caecum
☐ D   in the small bowel are often multiple
☐ E   of the appendix are usually benign

15. **Traumatic rupture of the oesophagus**

☐ A   may produce mediastinal emphysema
☐ B   may result in mediastinitis if left untreated
☐ C   is most easily diagnosed by oesophagoscopy
☐ D   when associated with blunt trauma is known as Boerhaave's syndrome
☐ E   when due to upper GI endoscopy usually occurs at the gastro-oesophageal junction

16. **Phaeochromocytomas**

☐ A   are benign in 20%
☐ B   in adults are extra-adrenal in 25% of cases
☐ C   in children are extra-adrenal in 10% of cases
☐ D   are bilateral in 5% of adults
☐ E   are bilateral in 25% in children
☐ F   produce clinical features as a result of increased secretion of catecholamines

17. **The following are recognised causes of leg ulceration in the gaiter region:**

□ A tuberculosis
□ B chronic venous insufficiency
□ C short saphenous vein incompetence
□ D ergot poisoning
□ E rheumatoid arthritis

18. **In vascular thrombosis**

□ A 'corraline clot' is also known as 'red thrombus'
□ B 'propagative clot' is also known as 'white thrombus'
□ C 'red thrombus' has little adherence to the vessel wall and is particularly likely to break up and form emboli
□ D anticoagulants have little effect on platelet aggregation
□ E thrombophlebitis is associated with a clinical inflammatory reaction

19. **Regarding cholecystectomy**

□ A unsuspected common bile duct calculi are present in approximately 10% of patients undergoing elective chole-cystectomy
□ B Calot's triangle is bordered by the cystic artery, the cystic duct, and the head of the pancreas
□ C choledocholithiasis is most commonly due to primary bile duct calculi
□ D the overall success rate of ERCP in extracting common bile duct calculi is approximately 50%

20. **Acute dislocations of the shoulder**

□ A are most frequently posterior
□ B with concomitant fractures of the greater tuberosity are very rare
□ C causing paraesthesia over the top of the shoulder suggest axillary nerve damage
□ D may be subsequent to an electric shock
□ E can occur as a result of a fall on the outstretched arm

21.   **In assessing the Glasgow Coma Scale in a patient with multiple injuries including a fractured left femur and a crush fracture of T8, the following statements are correct:**

☐ A   a history of drug abuse may affect the assessment
☐ B   response to movement is best assessed in the right lower limb
☐ C   a score of less than 8 implies 'coma' and a severe injury
☐ D   elective intubation will not affect the assessment
☐ E   extension in response to pain is a poor prognostic sign

22.   **Anal fissures**

☐ A   when chronic may be healed by GTN in 90% of cases
☐ B   may be treated by a partial surgical division of the external sphincter
☐ C   are associated with constipated stool
☐ D   are most common in the third and fourth decades of life

23.   **Regarding surgical anatomy of the thyroid gland**

☐ A   the thyroid gland has a definite fine capsule
☐ B   Berry's ligament connects the thyroid to the cricoid cartilage and upper trachea
☐ C   the inferior parathyroid glands are more constant in position than the superior parathyroid glands
☐ D   the middle thyroid veins are more constant in position than the superior and inferior thyroid veins
☐ E   unilateral recurrent laryngeal nerve division results in the contralateral vocal cord lying in the mid or cadaveric position

24.   **The internal jugular veins**

☐ A   emerge from the posterior compartment of the jugular foramen
☐ B   drain the cavernous dural venous sinus
☐ C   have the ansa cervicalis as an anterior relation
☐ D   are the most anterior structures in the carotid sheaths
☐ E   drain into the brachiocephalic veins behind the sternoclavicular joints

25. **The tongue**

- A   receives sensory innervation from the vagus nerve
- B   protrudes to the side of a unilateral lower motor nerve lesion
- C   is active during the voluntary phase of swallowing
- D   is retracted by the hyoglossus muscle
- E   contains lymphoid tissue

26. **The scalp**

- A   has an exclusive blood supply from branches of the external carotid artery
- B   contains the C1 dermatome
- C   is tightly attached to the cranium
- D   contains lymph nodes
- E   has a motor innervation from the facial nerve

27. **In the ante-cubital fossa the**

- A   median nerve lies lateral to the brachial artery
- B   brachial artery branches into radial and ulnar arteries
- C   posterior interosseous nerve may be found
- D   cephalic vein overlies the bicipital aponeurosis
- E   floor is formed by the head of the extensor digitorum superficialis muscle

28. **The fingers are extended after**

- A   contraction of the lumbrical muscles
- B   contraction of the interosseous muscles
- C   motor stimulation through the posterior cord of the brachial plexus
- D   motor stimulation through lateral digital branches of the median nerve
- E   motor stimulation through the ulnar nerve

27

29. The serratus anterior muscle

❑ A   has the thoracodorsal nerve deep to the fascia over its lateral surface
❑ B   rotates the scapula
❑ C   retracts the scapula
❑ D   receives its nerve supply from the upper trunk of the brachial plexus
❑ E   has most of its fibres inserted into the superior angle of the scapula

30. Compared with the lower end of the ileum, the upper end of the jejunum has

❑ A   a thicker wall
❑ B   less fat at the mesenteric border
❑ C   fewer circular folds
❑ D   a wider lumen
❑ E   fewer aggregated lymphatic follicles (Peyer's patches)

31. The right suprarenal gland

❑ A   lies against the bare area of the liver
❑ B   extends behind the inferior vena cava
❑ C   receives blood from the right inferior phrenic artery
❑ D   drains into the right renal vein
❑ E   lies on the 9th rib

32. The pancreas

❑ A   lies anterior to the right kidney
❑ B   lies in the trans-pyloric plane
❑ C   has an uncinate process lying anterior to the superior mesenteric vein
❑ D   gives attachment to the transverse mesocolon
❑ E   has the inferior mesenteric vein passing behind the neck

33. **Through the epiploic foramen the**

☐ A   caudate lobe of the liver is palpable in the lesser sac
☐ B   inferior vena cava lies posteriorly
☐ C   portal vein lies anteriorly
☐ D   right gastric artery lies posteriorly
☐ E   second part of the duodenum forms the lower boundary

34. **The male urethra**

☐ A   has a prostatic part bounded by internal and external urethral sphincter
☐ B   has a spongy part which, when ruptured, leaks urine over the abdomen subcutaneously
☐ C   has a 90° angle in its membranous part
☐ D   is narrowest at the external urethral meatus
☐ E   has a penile part invested by the erectile tissue of the corpora cavernosa

35. **The L3 vertebra**

☐ A   undergoes rotatory movements
☐ B   gives attachment to the left crus of the diaphragm
☐ C   is supplied by the internal iliac arteries
☐ D   has a vertebral foramen (central canal) enclosing the sacral segments of the spinal cord
☐ E   has a lateral process giving attachment to the iliolumbar ligament

36. **At the hip joint the**

☐ A   rectus femoris muscle is a flexor
☐ B   adductor magnus muscle is an extensor
☐ C   iliopsoas muscle is a lateral rotator
☐ D   tensor fascia lata muscle is a medial rotator
☐ E   ischiofemoral ligament limits flexion

37.   At the knee joint the

❑   A   popliteus tendon is intracapsular
❑   B   supra-patella bursa communicates with the joint
❑   C   iliotibial tract inserts into the fibula
❑   D   anterior cruciate ligament is supplied by the middle geniculate artery
❑   E   rotation occurs below the menisci

38.   On the dorsum of the foot the

❑   A   dorsalis pedis artery lies medial to the extensor hallucis longus tendon
❑   B   deep peroneal nerve lies medial to the dorsalis pedis artery
❑   C   L5 dermatome is present
❑   D   great saphenous vein lies anterior to the medial malleolus
❑   E   extensor retinaculum loops under the medial longitudinal arch

39.   The internal iliac artery supplies the

❑   A   sigmoid colon
❑   B   spinal cord
❑   C   trochanteric anastomosis
❑   D   cruciate anastomosis
❑   E   anterior superior iliac spine anastomosis

40.   Regarding groin hernias

❑   A   indirect inguinal hernias enter through the internal inguinal ring medial to the inferior epigastric vessels
❑   B   direct inguinal hernias usually emerge through the lateral aspect of the posterior wall of the inguinal canal
❑   C   sliding hernias have small bowel forming part of the wall of the sac
❑   D   femoral hernias are more common than inguinal hernias in women
❑   E   enlarging femoral hernias pass through the saphenous opening of the fascia lata, over the inguinal ligament, and into the subcutaneous tissues superficial to Scarpa's fascia

41.   An infant born at 32 weeks' gestation, weighing 1.2 kg

❑   A   always requires artificial ventilation for 24 hours after birth
❑   B   has a smaller insensible fluid loss than an adult
❑   C   may require placement of a central line in the internal jugular vein
❑   D   is at risk of necrotizing enterocolitis
❑   E   will not develop pyloric stenosis

42.   In exomphalos

❑   A   there is a 25% mortality rate after birth
❑   B   the herniated organs are covered by a membrane derived from the umbilical cord
❑   C   there is an association with trisomy 13
❑   D   the liver is rarely involved
❑   E   bowel can be inadvertently damaged by the cord clamp

43.   Hydrocele of infancy

❑   A   is usually of the 'communicating' variety
❑   B   should be left until the child is beyond 12 months of age before repair
❑   C   does not occur in females
❑   D   cannot be effectively treated by simple division of the patent processus vaginalis
❑   E   may not surround the testis

44.   Acute appendicitis in children

❑   A   can present as weight loss
❑   B   is uncommon in small infants
❑   C   can be difficult to diagnose under five years of age
❑   D   can be dealt with laparoscopically under ten years of age

45. Prostatic carcinoma

❑ A is the commonest male genito-urinary tract malignancy
❑ B has a constant incidence over the age of 65 years
❑ C presents with metastatic disease in over 50% of cases
❑ D androgen antagonists give symptomatic relief in disseminated carcinoma in only 30% of patients
❑ E is usually radiosensitive
❑ F surgical castration reduces circulating androgen levels by about 25%

46. Bladder cancer

❑ A is most commonly caused world-wide by exposure to chemical carcinogens
❑ B muscle-invasive bladder cancer is associated with abnormalities of chromosome 17
❑ C carcinoma in situ has a better prognosis than superficial papillary tumours ($G1_pT_a$)
❑ D treatment of most bladder tumours is by cystectomy
❑ E orthotopic bladder reconstruction is contraindicated in patients with impaired renal function

47. Undescended testis (UDT)

❑ A occurs in 1% of term infants
❑ B will descend in 75% of cases by the first year of life
❑ C placement within the scrotum should be undertaken by one year of age
❑ D placement within the scrotum reduces the risk of subsequent tumour development
❑ E is best located with CT scanning when in a suspected intra-abdominal position

48. **The following drugs may be used in the treatment of benign prostatic hypertrophy:**

□ A tamsulosin
□ B alfuzosin
□ C tolterodine
□ D finasteride
□ E goserelin

49. **The following tumours are associated with the given risk factors:**

□ A scrotal carcinoma and chimney sweeps
□ B bladder cancer and dye workers
□ C renal transitional cell carcinoma and phenacetin abuse
□ D penile cancer and circumcision
□ E prostate cancer and vasectomy

50. **Rigid ureteroscopy**

□ A may be diagnostic or therapeutic
□ B is associated with a 3% incidence of ureteric strictures
□ C is routinely performed in annual surveillance of the upper tracts in patients with superficial bladder cancer
□ D sterilisation of instruments is performed using ethylene oxide

51. **Torsion of the testis**

□ A can be excluded by colour Doppler ultrasound
□ B when found at exploration, should always have the contra-lateral testis fixed
□ C is most commonly seen between 8 and 10 years of age
□ D the testis may be viable after 24 hours
□ E is usually extra-vaginal when occurring in adolescents

52. **In Hirschsprung's disease**

- ❏ A there is absent sympathetic nerve supply to the bowel
- ❏ B there is frequent distal rectal sparing
- ❏ C there is a male predominance
- ❏ D the lumen of the aganglionic segment is grossly dilated
- ❏ E enterocolitis may be a complication

SECTION 2 – EMQs

Theme: Rectal bleeding

A   Crohn's disease
B   Solitary juvenile polyp
C   Familial adenomatous polyposis
D   Necrotising enterocolitis (NEC)
E   Intussusception
F   Fissure in ano
G   Meckel's diverticulum
H   Mid-gut volvulus

For each of the clinical scenarios below, select the most likely cause of rectal bleeding from the list above. Each option may be used once, more than once or not at all.

☐   61.   A 7-year-old girl with weight loss and anaemia
☐   62.   A 13-year-old boy with lower abdominal pain and shock
☐   63.   A 3-year-old boy with painless bleeding, mixed with stool
☐   64.   A 13-year-old girl with painless bleeding, mixed with stool, whose father died of colorectal cancer aged 35
☐   65.   A 10-month-old collapsed girl with a previous history of intermittent bilestained vomiting

Theme: Surgical investigations

A   Gastrografin enema
B   Abdominal and pelvic CT scan
C   Small bowel follow-through
D   ERCP
E   Abdominal and pelvic ultrasound
F   Colonoscopy
G   Barium enema

For each of the conditions listed below, select the most appropriate investigation from the list above. Each option may be used once, more than once, or not at all.

☐   66.   A suspected acutely obstructing large bowel cancer
☐   67.   Empyema of the gall bladder
☐   68.   Colonic diverticular abscess
☐   69.   Terminal ileal Crohn's disease
☐   70.   Colonic anastomotic leak on day 4 post-operatively

Theme: Side-effects of treatment for inflammatory bowel disease

A   Sulphasalazine
B   Corticosteroids
C   Methotrexate
D   Azathioprine
E   Metronidazole

For each of the options listed below, select the most likely associated side-effects from the list of drugs above. Each option may be used once, more than once, or not at all.

☐   71.   Irreversible peripheral neuropathy
☐   72.   Reversible infertility due to oligospermia
☐   73.   Osteoporosis
☐   74.   Cataracts
☐   75.   Hepatic fibrosis
☐   76.   Pneumonitis

Theme: Parathyroid glands

A   Inferior parathyroid glands
B   Superior parathyroid glands

For each of the statements below, select the correct anatomical structure from the list above. Each option may be used once, more than once, or not at all.

☐ 77. Most lie adjacent to the cricothyroid notch close to the recurrent laryngeal nerve
☐ 78. When ectopic, may lie in the posterior mediastinum
☐ 79. Are derived from the third branchial pouch
☐ 80. May lie anywhere from the mandible to the anterior mediastinum
☐ 81. Are derived from the fourth branchial pouch
☐ 82. 20% lie on or within the supra-sternal portion of the thymus

Theme: Anatomy of joints in the head and neck

A   Atlanto-occipital
B   Temporo-mandibular
C   Intervertebral disc
D   Cricothyroid
E   Sterno-clavicular
F   Crico-arytenoid
G   Atlanto-axial

For each of the statements below, select the most likely joint from the list above. Each option may be used once, more than once, or not at all.

☐ 83. Movements at the joint lengthen the vocal cords
☐ 84. Is a secondary cartilaginous joint
☐ 85. Subserves a rotatory movement whose axis is outside the joint
☐ 86. At which flexion of the head occurs
☐ 87. Has a fibrocartilagenous intra-articular disc
☐ 88. Stabilised by a transverse ligament
☐ 89. Is a saddle joint

Theme: Surface/radiological anatomy of the anterior abdominal wall

A   Trans-pyloric plane
B   L4 vertebral body
C   L5 vertebral body
D   Mid inguinal point
E   Above and medial to the pubic tubercle
F   Sacro-iliac joint
G   Below and lateral to the pubic tubercle
H   Mid point of inguinal ligament
I   Umbilicus
J   12th rib
K   10th rib
L   Trans-tubercular plane

For each of the statements below, select the most likely option from the list above. Each option may be used once, more than once, or not at all.

☐   90.   Division of the aorta into the common iliac vessels
☐   91.   Ureter
☐   92.   Femoral artery
☐   93.   Upper poles of the kidneys
☐   94.   External ring of the femoral canal
☐   95.   L5 vertebral body
☐   96.   Termination of the spinal cord
☐   97.   Spleen

Theme: Nerve damage

A   Horner's syndrome
B   Posterior interosseus nerve lesion
C   Median nerve neurapraxia
D   Neurapraxia of the common peroneal nerve
E   Neurotmesis of the common peroneal nerve
F   Sciatic nerve injury
G   Radial nerve neurapraxia
H   Radial nerve neurotmesis

For each of the patients listed below, select the site and type of nerve damage that best explains the clinical situation from the list above. Each option may be used once, more than once, or not at all.

☐ 98. A 21-year-old man sustained a comminuted fracture of the right femur and a fracture of the ipsilateral tibia and fibula. He was treated with skeletal traction and a below knee POP overnight. On review it was noticed that he could not dorsiflex his toes on the right foot.

☐ 99. Which nerve is commonly damaged in a child with a severely displaced supracondylar fracture of the humerus and what type of damage occurs?

☐ 100. Following a difficult elective operative procedure plating a non-union of the humeral shaft, the patient was unable to extend the fingers and wrist. No nerves were visualised during the procedure.

☐ 101. A motorcyclist came off his bike at considerable speed. Both he and his bike were then dragged down the road by a car. On examination he had a flail left upper limb.

☐ 102. Following a total hip replacement performed via the posterior approach, the patient was noted to have a foot drop.

Theme: Imaging

A   Plain KUB
B   IVU
C   Ultrasound
D   Cystogram
E   Retrograde ureterogram
F   DMSA scan
G   DTPA scan
H   CT scan

For each of the patients below, select the most appropriate treatment from the list above. Each option may be used once, more than once or not at all.

☐   103. A 34-year-old obese male presents with a sudden onset of colicky right loin pain radiating to his groin. He has microscopic haematuria. He has a history of severe anaphylaxis with intravenous contrast. An ultrasound scan is unhelpful due to his obesity.

☐   104. A 45-year-old female has a right staghorn calculus on plain KUB. An IVU shows this kidney fails to excrete contrast. An ultrasound scan shows the kidney has a thin parenchyma without evidence of hydronephrosis.

☐   105. A 22-year-old female presents with a history of left loin pain shortly after drinking alcohol. An ultrasound scan shows hydronephrosis with a normal calibre ureter. An IVU shows a narrowing at the pelviureteric junction.

END OF SYSTEM PAPER 2

SYSTEM PAPER 3
SECTION 1 – MCQS

1.   **Anaplastic thyroid carcinoma**

❑   A   has a 90% one year survival
❑   B   has a similar clinical presentation to lymphoma
❑   C   may invade the carotid artery
❑   D   is usually cured by aggressive surgery
❑   E   commonly involves the recurrent laryngeal nerve

2.   **Complications of submandibular gland excision include**

❑   A   weakness of the angle of the mouth
❑   B   anaesthesia of the contralateral half of the tongue
❑   C   deviation of the tongue to the contralateral side
❑   D   Frey's syndrome
❑   E   damage to the retromandibular vein

3.   **The normal function of the colon is in the absorption of**

❑   A   water
❑   B   sodium
❑   C   chloride
❑   D   bicarbonate
❑   E   bile salts

4.   **Raised serum amylase levels may occur in the following conditions:**

❑   A   acute cholecystitis
❑   B   hyperosmolar crisis
❑   C   carcinoid syndrome
❑   D   intestinal strangulation
❑   E   renal failure

5.   **In colonic diverticular disease**

☐   A   Asians have an increased incidence of left-sided disease
☐   B   the diverticula are antimesenteric
☐   C   the diverticula are true rather than pulsion types
☐   D   the circular muscle of the affected bowel is thickened
☐   E   the affected bowel is usually elongated

6.   **Long-term effects of gastrectomy include**

☐   A   low serum iron
☐   B   renal calculi
☐   C   osteomalacia
☐   D   vitamin B_{12} deficiency
☐   E   vitamin C deficiency

7.   **Full thickness rectal prolapse**

☐   A   has an equal sex incidence
☐   B   tends to occur at the extremes of life
☐   C   usually starts as an internal intussusception
☐   D   may be treated by direct suturing to the sacrum
☐   E   may cause faecal incontinence

8.   **Carcinoid tumours**

☐   A   may be found incidentally
☐   B   most commonly occur in the large bowel
☐   C   are neuroendocrine in origin
☐   D   secrete bradykinin
☐   E   may be treated with chemo-embolization

9.   Hepatic metastases from colorectal cancer

❑   A   are potentially curable in 25% of cases if completely excised
          in the absence of other metastatic or recurrent disease
❑   B   best surgical results are achieved by resection along hepatic
          segmental lines
❑   C   are not curable using chemo-therapeutic regimens
❑   D   are present in about 10% of patients at the time of diagnosis of
          the primary tumour
❑   E   are radiosensitive

10.   Colorectal cancer

❑   A   is inherited in approximately 40% of cases
❑   B   is metachronous in 10% of cases
❑   C   is synchronous in 5% of cases
❑   D   inevitably occurs in cases of untreated FAP
❑   E   clinical stage of disease is the most important prognostic factor

11.   Barium enema examination of the colon

❑   A   is as sensitive as colonoscopy for the assessment of polyps
❑   B   is more sensitive than colonoscopy for the assessment of
          diverticular disease
❑   C   can exclude collagenous colitis
❑   D   single contrast studies are superior to double contrast studies
          in the detection of mucosal abnormalities
❑   E   is accurate for the assessment of appendiceal pathology
❑   F   has a lower major complication rate than colonoscopy

12.   Acute acalculous cholecystitis

❑   A   accounts for approximately 10% of cases of acute cholecystitis
❑   B   is especially common after colonic surgery
❑   C   is thought to be related to supersaturation of bile
❑   D   clinical signs may be overshadowed by concomitant illness
❑   E   is diagnosed by full thickness gall bladder biopsy

13. Inflammatory bowel disease (IBD)

- A Crohn's disease has a much higher prevalence than ulcerative colitis in Western populations
- B cases have risen over the past four decades
- C is most common in early adult life
- D has a higher prevalence in the lower social classes
- E has a higher incidence in Jews living outside Israel

14. The approximate incidences of Crohn's disease involvement are

- A ileocaecal only – 40%
- B colon only – 25%
- C ileum only – 10%
- D extensive small bowel disease – 30%
- E miscellaneous (e.g. confined to the anorectum, oral, gastric) – 2%

15. Surgical techniques of preserving the traumatised spleen include

- A omental patch repair
- B topical thrombogenic agents
- C wrapping with a Dexon mesh
- D induced hypotension to minimise haemorrhage
- E partial splenectomy

16. Concerning lumps in the groin

- A the neck of a femoral hernia is located above and lateral to pubic tubercle
- B enlarged inguinal lymph nodes give rise to a cough impulse
- C varicoceles are usually tender
- D clinical examination enables the examiner to 'get above' the lump if the lesion is a cyst of the canal of Nuck
- E a hydrocele of the cord is clinically irreducible

17. **Child's classification of hepato-cellular function in cirrhosis includes**

❏ A serum bilirubin
❏ B serum calcium
❏ C white cell count
❏ D core body temperature
❏ E the presence of ascites

18. **Cholesterol gallstones**

❏ A usually contain a pigmented centre
❏ B account for approximately 25% of all gallstones
❏ C are visible on AXR in 50% of cases
❏ D are more common in sickle cell disease
❏ E are usually soft and smooth bordered

19. **The following are causes of leg lymphoedema:**

❏ A familial predisposition
❏ B angio-oedema
❏ C *Wuchereria bancrofti* infection
❏ D radiotherapy
❏ E Klippel-Trenaunay syndrome

20. **Indications for right carotid endarterectomy include**

❏ A TIAs affecting the right face, arm and leg with 80% right internal carotid artery stenosis
❏ B right eye amaurosis fugax with 90% right internal carotid artery stenosis
❏ C left completed stroke 35 days ago, with good recovery and 95% internal right carotid artery stenosis
❏ D no symptoms but occluded right carotid artery and 90% left internal carotid artery stenosis
❏ E left facial TIAs and dysphasia with 50% right internal carotid artery stenosis

21.   The right common carotid artery

❑ A   bifurcates at the level of the upper border of the cricoid
          cartilage
❑ B   is a branch of the aortic arch
❑ C   has the cervical sympathetic chain as an anterior relation
❑ D   lies lateral to the lateral lobe of the thyroid gland
❑ E   is separated from the phrenic nerve by prevertebral fascia

22.   On turning the head to the left

❑ A   the left sternocleidomastoid muscle is the main agonist
❑ B   movement takes place at the atlanto-occipital joint
❑ C   impulses pass via the spinal accessory nerve
❑ D   the axis of rotation runs vertically through the odontoid
          process
❑ E   movement is limited by the typical cervical vertebrae

23.   The palatine tonsillar bed

❑ A   lies in the oral cavity
❑ B   is floored by the middle constrictor muscle
❑ C   contains the superior pharyngeal nerve
❑ D   is pierced by branches of the facial artery
❑ E   is drained by the external palatine vein

24.   The Eustachian tube

❑ A   drains the inner ear
❑ B   pierces the pharyngobasilar fascia
❑ C   gives attachment to the tensor veli palatini muscle
❑ D   can be obstructed by an enlarging palatine tonsil
❑ E   closes during swallowing

25. **The true vocal folds are**

☐ A lined by respiratory epithelium
☐ B formed by the lower free edge of the quadrangular membranes
☐ C abducted by the lateral cricoarytenoid muscles
☐ D innervated by sensory fibres of the internal laryngeal nerves
☐ E tensed by contractions of the cricothyroid muscles

26. **The basilic vein**

☐ A begins on the medial side of the dorsal venous arch
☐ B drains into the subclavian vein
☐ C is accompanied by the medial cutaneous nerve of the forearm
☐ D pierces the deep fascia in the arm
☐ E lies medial to the biceps tendon in the cubital fossa

27. **During full abduction of the arm the following muscles are active:**

☐ A infraspinatus
☐ B trapezius
☐ C supraspinatus
☐ D serratus anterior
☐ E teres major

28. **The scaphoid bone**

☐ A articulates with the radius
☐ B is palpable in the 'snuffbox'
☐ C has a vascular supply penetrating its distal surface
☐ D gives attachment to the flexor retinaculum
☐ E gives attachment to the adductor pollicis muscle

29. **The knee joint is locked by**

☐ A medial rotation of the femur on the tibia
☐ B contraction of the popliteus muscle
☐ C tensing of the oblique popliteal ligament
☐ D the anchorage of the medial femoral condyle by the anterior cruciate ligament
☐ E contraction of the tensor fascia lata muscle

30. **In the lumbosacral plexus the**

☐ A sympathetic trunk sends grey rami to all roots
☐ B parasympathetic nerves originate from S2/3 spinal segments
☐ C lumbosacral trunk lies on the piriformis muscle
☐ D lumbosacral trunk underlies the common iliac vessels
☐ E posterior divisions of anterior rami supply the adductor muscles

31. **The patella reflex is**

☐ A lost after femoral nerve transection
☐ B mediated through the posterior divisions of anterior rami of lumbar nerves
☐ C lost following T12 cord transection
☐ D present after L2–4 dorsal root avulsions
☐ E absent after dorsal column demyelination

32. **The ilioinguinal nerve**

☐ A lies posterior to the kidney
☐ B is entirely sensory
☐ C passes through the deep inguinal ring
☐ D supplies sensation to the scrotum
☐ E may be damaged by a gridiron incision

33. **The linea semilunaris of the rectus sheath**

- ❑ A   is crossed by the inferior epigastric vessels
- ❑ B   has an upper attachment overlying the liver
- ❑ C   is one of the preferred lines of incision in abdominal surgery
- ❑ D   is formed by interdigitation of the internal and external oblique aponeuroses
- ❑ E   is crossed by the medial umbilical ligament

34. **The processus vaginalis**

- ❑ A   is formed by visceral peritoneum
- ❑ B   forms a sac in which the testis descends through the inguinal canal
- ❑ C   when present in adults, predisposes to direct inguinal hernia
- ❑ D   forms the tunica vaginalis in the adult
- ❑ E   invests the adult vas deferens

35. **In the bony pelvis the**

- ❑ A   sacral cornua are palpable per rectum
- ❑ B   pubic tubercles are palpable lateral to the external ring of the inguinal canal
- ❑ C   femoral canals lie medial to the lacunar ligaments
- ❑ D   sacral spines are palpable per vaginum
- ❑ E   trans-tubercular plane passes through the spinous process of the L3 vertebra

36. **The radiological features of osteoarthritis are**

- ❑ A   an increase in the joint space due to synovial fluid production
- ❑ B   bony sclerosis
- ❑ C   cyst formation in the weight bearing portion of the joint
- ❑ D   osteophyte formation at the joint margin
- ❑ E   erosions in the periarticular region

37. **The mesentery of the small bowel**

- [ ] A contains veins which drain into the inferior vena cava
- [ ] B has a root overlying the left sacroiliac joint
- [ ] C contains post-ganglionic fibres of the vagus nerve
- [ ] D contains arteries that supply large bowel
- [ ] E overlies the transverse mesocolon

38. **The diseased enlarging ovary**

- [ ] A may extend into the recto-uterine pouch
- [ ] B refers pain to the skin over the anterior aspect of the thigh
- [ ] C drains lymph into the para-aortic lymph nodes
- [ ] D constricts the ureter
- [ ] E may be palpable per vaginum

39. **In a patient with a prolapsed L5/S1 intervertebral disc**

- [ ] A the history of trauma may be minimal
- [ ] B pain radiating to the buttocks implies nerve root involvement
- [ ] C pain radiating down to the ankle on coughing and sneezing implies nerve root involvement
- [ ] D urinary retention can be secondary to pain and bed rest
- [ ] E an absent ankle jerk means that the disc should be removed

40. **The following conditions are recognised causes of avascular necrosis in the absence of injury:**

- [ ] A sickle cell disease
- [ ] B haemophilia A
- [ ] C Hunter's disease
- [ ] D Gaucher's disease
- [ ] E decompression sickness

41. **Osteochondritis in the upper limb may be found in the absence of injury in the**

❑ A scaphoid
❑ B lunate
❑ C humeral head
❑ D capitulum
❑ E metacarpal heads

42. **In gastroschisis**

❑ A the baby should be delivered by Caesarean section
❑ B the baby may require total parenteral nutrition for several weeks
❑ C the bowel is covered by a membrane derived from the umbilical cord
❑ D chromosomal abnormalities are common
❑ E it may be necessary to correct the abnormality using a 'silo' (silastic pouch)

43. **Inguinal hernia in infancy**

❑ A is usually of the direct variety
❑ B is more common in babies born prematurely
❑ C can safely be left until the child weighs over 10 kg
❑ D does not routinely require a herniorrhaphy
❑ E is not associated with a patent processus vaginalis

44. **Bile stained vomiting is a feature of**

❑ A mid-gut volvulus
❑ B pyloric stenosis
❑ C intussusception
❑ D oesophageal atresia
❑ E gastro-oesophageal reflux

45. Positions for an ectopic testis include

- ❏ A   inguinal
- ❏ B   penile
- ❏ C   intra-abdominal
- ❏ D   femoral
- ❏ E   high scrotal

46. In the staging of prostate cancer

- ❏ A   biopsy may detect stage $T1_c$ prostate cancer
- ❏ B   seminal vesical involvement is stage $T3_a$
- ❏ C   tumour detected following TURP is stage $T1_a$ if < 15% chips involved
- ❏ D   palpable tumour involving both lobes is $T2_b$
- ❏ E   extra capsular extension, not involving seminal vesicals, is $T3_b$

47. Concerning surgery for muscle-invasive bladder cancer

- ❏ A   the usual treatment in males is cystoprostatectomy and ileal conduit
- ❏ B   the finding of an organ confined prostate cancer is a contra-indication to orthotopic bladder reconstruction
- ❏ C   it may be cured by TURBT alone in approximately 10% of cases
- ❏ D   trans-urethral prostate biopsies must be taken in males prior to orthotopic bladder reconstruction to exclude prostatic carcinoma-in-situ
- ❏ E   curative cystectomy is contraindicated if the pre-op CT shows lymph node involvement

48. Causes of macroscopic haematuria are

- ❏ A   bladder diverticulum
- ❏ B   renal TB
- ❏ C   renal tract calculus
- ❏ D   benign prostatic hypertrophy (BPH)
- ❏ E   suprapubic catheterization

49. A 25-year-old male was kicked in the groin during a football match. He noticed a persistent hard, painless swelling in his scrotum. On examination a hard irregular lump is found at the lower pole of his testis. His GP has sent an α-fetoprotein level which is markedly elevated. The following investigation(s)/treatment(s) are indicated:

- A   scrotal ultrasound
- B   CT abdomen
- C   chest X-ray
- D   abdominal X-ray
- E   abdominal ultrasound
- F   incision and drainage of haematoma
- G   radical inguinal orchidectomy

50. A 51-year-old male presents with acute urinary retention. The following immediate investigations/treatments are required:

- A   suprapubic catheterization if history of recent frank haematuria
- B   measurement of urea, electrolytes and creatinine
- C   measurement of PSA
- D   renal ultrasound
- E   urine cytology

51. Extracorporeal shock-wave lithotripsy (ESWL)

- A   is contraindicated in pregnancy
- B   is contraindicated in children
- C   can cause Steinstrasse
- D   piezoceramic machines are safe in patients with pacemakers
- E   pre-treatment insertion of a ureteric stent is recommended if the stone bulk is > 1.5 cm

52.   Bladder calculi

☐   A   are usually secondary to bladder outlet obstruction
☐   B   are associated with upper urinary tract calculi in 15–20% cases
☐   C   are most commonly composed of calcium oxalate
☐   D   usually present with obstructive rather than irritative symptoms
☐   E   can be diagnosed by a simple urine test

SECTION 2 – EMQs

Theme: Jaundice

A   Pre-hepatic jaundice
B   Hepatic jaundice
C   Post-hepatic jaundice

For each of the clinical findings given below, select the correct type of jaundice from the list above. Each option may be used once, more than once, or not at all.

☐   61.   Bilirubin in the urine
☐   62.   History of recent foreign travel
☐   63.   Positive Courvoisier's sign
☐   64.   Associated pancreatitis
☐   65.   Pruritus
☐   66.   Intake of hepatotoxic drugs
☐   67.   History of fever, rigors and sweats

Theme: Anatomy of abdominal vasculature

A   Inferior mesenteric vein
B   Superior mesenteric vein
C   Left gastric vein
D   Right renal artery
E   Left renal vein
F   Gastroduodenal artery
G   Portal vein
H   Supra-renal artery
I   Left colic artery
J   Ileocolic artery
K   Splenic artery
L   Middle colic artery

For each of the statements below, select the most likely option from the list above. Each option may be used once, more than once, or not at all.

☐   68.   Porto-systemic anastomosis
☐   69.   Lies posterior to the first part of the duodenum
☐   70.   Drains into the splenic vein
☐   71.   Lies posterior to the inferior vena cava
☐   72.   Drains the suprarenal gland
☐   73.   Supplies the caecum
☐   74.   Lies to the left of the superior mesenteric ~~vein~~ artery
☐   75.   Supplies the fundus of the stomach

Theme: Anatomy of the inguinal canal

A   Anterior wall
B   Roof
C   Posterior wall
D   Floor

For each of the combinations of structures listed below, select the most appropriate portion of the inguinal canal they form from the list above. Each option may be used once, more than once, or not at all.

☐   76.   Inguinal and lacunar ligaments
☐   77.   Internal oblique and the aponeurosis of the external oblique
☐   78.   Conjoint tendon and fascia transversalis
☐   79.   Internal oblique and transversus abdominus muscles

Theme: Anatomy of joints in the upper limb

A   Shoulder
B   Elbow
C   Superior radio-ulnar
D   Inferior radio-ulnar
E   Wrist
F   Interphalangeal
G   Carpometacarpal
H   Acromioclavicular

For each of the descriptions below, select the most likely anatomical joint from the list above. Each option may be used once, more than once, or not at all.

☐   80.   Has an intra-articular ligament coursing through the joint
☐   81.   Is a saddle joint
☐   82.   Is stabilised by an annular ligament
☐   83.   Movements at this distal joint are the reciprocal to those at the proximal joint
☐   84.   Is an articulation between three bones
☐   85.   Has collateral ligaments which limit extension
☐   86.   Has an articular disc included in the proximal articulating surface

Theme: Bone Disease

A   Paget's Disease
B   Avascular necrosis
C   Rickets
D   Osteomalacia
E   Osteoarthritis
F   Osteosarcoma
G   Osteochondroma

For each of the clinical scenarios given below, select the most likely diagnosis from the list above. Each option may be used once, more than once, or not at all.

❑   87.   A patient with a successful renal transplant presents with severe hip pain. She had been treated with immunosuppressive drugs and steroids for many years prior to her transplant ten years ago.

❑   88.   A boy aged 15, was kicked playing football and ever since then he has been aware that his lower thigh has been painful and swollen. Examination confirmed a degree of diffuse swelling and tenderness around the distal femur with a small effusion within the knee joint and noticeable muscle wasting.

❑   89.   A toddler aged two, was referred for advice regarding his bow-legs. These were considered to be within normal limits for his age but he was also noted to be of short stature and had a past medical history which included a period of 'failure to thrive'. This, however, appeared to improve on monitoring without need for formal investigation.

❑   90.   A 60-year-old man comes to clinic asking for advice regarding his 'bent' legs. The history was difficult to elicit because of his deafness, but it appeared that the legs had become progressively deformed over the last few years although with little in the way of pain.

❑   91.   A 22-year-old man wanted advice regarding a lump in the axilla which was bony, hard and non-tender. He thought that it had been present for many years and there had been no change in the condition recently. Thorough examination confirmed the presence of several bony swellings in the metaphyseal region of several bones.

Theme: Renal tract calculi

A ESWL
B Percutaneous nephrostomy
C Nephrectomy
D Percutaneous nephrolithotomy
E Ureteroscopy
F Conservative management

For each of the patients below, select the most appropriate treatment from the list above. Each option may be used once, more than once or not at all.

☐ 92. A 24-year-old female presents with intermittent right loin pain. MSU confirms microscopic haematuria. A plain radiograph shows a 1.2 cm calculus in the region of the right kidney. An IVU confirms that it lies within the renal pelvis but not causing obstruction.

☐ 93. A 45-year-old female presents with a history of recurrent UTIs and chronic left loin pain. An ultrasound shows a large echogenic mass in the left pelvi-calyceal system. A plain KUB demonstrates a staghorn calculus. A DMSA scan shows differential split function Left:Right, 9:91.

☐ 94. A 31-year-old male presents with colicky left loin pain. He is tachycardic, flushed and has a temperature of 38.5°C. An IVU shows a 3 mm calculus in the mid-ureter.

Theme: Colorectal surgery

A   Left hemicolectomy
B   Transverse loop colostomy
C   Anterior resection
D   Pan-proctocolectomy
E   Sub-total colectomy
F   Abdomino-perineal resection
G   Ileo-colonic bypass
H   Hartmann's procedure
I   Sigmoid colectomy and primary anastomosis

For each of the patients described below, select the most appropriate surgical option from the list above. Each option may be used once, more than once, or not at all.

❑   95.   A 55-year-old man re-attends the surgical Outpatient Department with bleeding from the back passage. He has recently completed a course of chemoradiotherapy for a squamous anal carcinoma. He underwent an EUA which revealed some residual tumour.

❑   96.   A 30-year-old lady with known ulcerative colitis, is admitted as an emergency with abdominal distension, vomiting, rectal bleeding and dehydration. She undergoes a course of conservative medical management but does not respond to steroids and immunosuppressive therapy. Her albumin is 20 g/l, WBC 25 x 10^9/l and her colonic diameter on AXR is 9 cm.

❑   97.   A 45-year-old man is admitted as an emergency to the Accident & Emergency Department with generalised peritonitis. Following aggressive resuscitation he is taken to the operating theatre where a hard 4 cm mass in the sigmoid colon is found. There is gross faecal contamination of the peritoneal cavity. His liver has one umbilicated nodule in the left lobe. The rest of the laparotomy is normal.

Theme: Abdominal disease

A   Crohn's disease
B   Diverticular disease
C   Ulcerative colitis
D   Familial adenomatous polyposis
E   Peutz–Jeghers syndrome

For each of the following conditions below, select the most likely associated disease from the list above. Each option may be used once, more than once, or not at all.

☐ 98.   Intra-abdominal desmoids
☐ 99.   Ankylosing spondylitis
☐ 100. Enteroenteric fistulae
☐ 101. Perianal sepsis
☐ 102. Pyoderma gangrenosum
☐ 103. Colovesical fistula

END OF SYSTEM PAPER 3

SYSTEM PAPER 4
SECTION 1 – MCQS

1. **Complications of otitis media include**

❑ A   papilloedema
❑ B   facial nerve paralysis
❑ C   cerebellar abscess
❑ D   homonymous hemianopia
❑ E   sudden deafness

2. **The posterior triangle of the neck contains the**

❑ A   great auricular nerve
❑ B   omohyoid muscle
❑ C   supraclavicular nerves
❑ D   roots of the brachial plexus
❑ E   vertebral artery

3. **The chorda tympani nerve**

❑ A   contains taste fibres
❑ B   is secretomotor to the parotid salivary gland
❑ C   is surgically accessible on the tympanic membrane
❑ D   is vulnerable to damage during parotid surgery
❑ E   is damaged by compression at the stylomastoid foramen

4. **Medullary thyroid cancer**

❑ A   is familial in the majority of cases
❑ B   is associated with Multiple Endocrine Neoplasia Type II
❑ C   often presents with palpable lymph node metastases
❑ D   produces carcino-embryonic antigen
❑ E   cannot be diagnosed by fine needle aspiration cytology

5. **Ludwig's angina**

☐ A   is usually caused by an infected tooth
☐ B   may cause dysphagia
☐ C   should be regarded as a surgical emergency
☐ D   is treated with oral amoxycillin
☐ E   is caused by peptostreptococcus

6. **The nasopharynx**

☐ A   receives a sensory nerve supply from the glossopharyngeal nerve
☐ B   contains the pharyngeal tonsil
☐ C   is ridged by the palatopharyngeal fold
☐ D   has the internal carotid artery lying against its wall
☐ E   contains the pyramidal fossa

7. **Lateral swellings of the neck include**

☐ A   cervical ribs
☐ B   thyroglossal cysts
☐ C   pharyngeal pouches
☐ D   carotid body tumours (chemodectomas)
☐ E   laryngocoeles

8. **Elevated parathyroid hormone produces**

☐ A   increased gastric acid secretion
☐ B   raised plasma albumin
☐ C   increased calcium excretion in the urine
☐ D   increased phosphate excretion in the urine
☐ E   tetany

9.   **Transection of the anterior division of the mandibular nerve (Vc) in the infratemporal fossa results in**

❑ A ipsilateral paralysis of the buccinator muscle
❑ B dysphagia
❑ C ipsilateral anaesthesia of the mandibular teeth
❑ D deviation of the jaw to the side of the lesion on protrusion
❑ E ipsilateral anaesthesia of the mucosa of the oral vestibule

10.   **Meckel's diverticulum**

❑ A is a remnant of the umbilical vein
❑ B lies on the antimesenteric border of the small bowel
❑ C is supplied by a terminal branch of the superior mesenteric artery
❑ D is a pulsion diverticulum
❑ E containing ectopic gastric epithelium may cause ulceration
❑ F most commonly causes an inflammatory complication

11.   **Gallstone ileus**

❑ A usually follows iatrogenic fistulation of the gall bladder into the gastrointestinal tract
❑ B calculi usually impact in the proximal ileum
❑ C usually produces complete obstruction
❑ D may produce air in the biliary tree visible on AXR
❑ E is most common in the < 60 year age group

12.   **The following are causes of arm lymphoedema:**

❑ A axillary surgery
❑ B axillary vein thrombosis
❑ C lymphangioma
❑ D axillary radiotherapy
❑ E carcinoma of the breast

QUESTIONS – System Paper 4

63

13. **The following have an association with duodenal ulcers:**

☐ A *H. pylori* infection
☐ B blood group A
☐ C excess acid pepsin secretion
☐ D chronic sucralfate ingestion
☐ E smoking

14. **Indications for a CT scan following a head injury include**

☐ A fluctuating consciousness
☐ B falling blood pressure and bradycardia
☐ C periorbital haematoma
☐ D focal neurology
☐ E a skull fracture on X-ray

15. **Typical endoscopic features of Crohn's disease include**

☐ A aphthous ulceration
☐ B pseudomembranes
☐ C loss of the normal vascular pattern
☐ D deep fissuring ulceration with a cobblestone appearance
☐ E microadenomas

16. **In the surgical treatment of rectal cancer**

☐ A distal intra-mural spread is often 3 cm
☐ B a distal resection clearance of 5 cm from the rectal tumour is mandatory
☐ C the mesorectum contains an abundance of lymphatic tissue
☐ D irrigation of the divided bowel ends with cytotoxic solutions and reduces local tumour recurrence
☐ E exfoliated malignant cells may be present intraluminally, adjacent to transection lines at the time of surgery

17.   **Borders of Hesselbach's triangle include**

- A   the inferior epigastric artery
- B   the inguinal ligament
- C   the medial border of the rectus abdominis muscle
- D   lacunar ligament
- E   the femoral artery

18.   **Epigastric hernias**

- A   are often multiple
- B   usually contain small bowel
- C   are frequently irreducible
- D   are often more easily seen than felt
- E   usually require a mesh repair

19.   **Typical radiological features of acute ulcerative colitis on plain AXR include**

- A   loss of haustrations
- B   mucosal irregularity
- C   left-sided faecal loading
- D   a 'beak' sign
- E   absence of faecal residue within the actively inflamed part of the colon

20.   **In investigations for inflammatory bowel disease**

- A   endoscopic visual appearances alone allow a definitive diagnosis between ulcerative colitis and Crohn's disease
- B   an 'instant' enema is one that is performed without bowel preparation
- C   mucosal granularity on an 'instant' enema suggests at least mild inflammation
- D   colonoscopy during a disease 'flare' is associated with an increased risk of perforation
- E   proximal colonic stool on plain AXR in a patient with ulcerative colitis suggests that the proximal large bowel is significantly inflamed

21. **In colorectal cancer**

☐ A   the incidence of invasive cancer in colorectal polyps < 1 cm in size is approximately 10%
☐ B   the incidence of invasive cancer in colorectal polyps 1–2 cm in size is approximately 35%
☐ C   the incidence of invasive cancer in colorectal polyps > 2 cm in size is approximately 80%
☐ D   villous adenomas have a greater risk of malignant change than tubular adenomas of the same size

22. **The inferior mesenteric vein**

☐ A   drains the rectum
☐ B   lies anterior to the left renal vein
☐ C   is a tributary of the portal vein
☐ D   lies to the right of the inferior mesenteric artery
☐ E   lies anterior to the left ureter

23. **The lesser omentum**

☐ A   is supplied by gastroepiploic arteries
☐ B   is attached to the liver in the fissure of the ligamentum venosum
☐ C   encloses the right gastric vessels
☐ D   has the common hepatic bile duct in its free edge
☐ E   is attached to the first part of the duodenum

24. **Anorectal lesions associated with HIV-infected patients include**

☐ A   Kaposi's sarcoma
☐ B   apocrine hidrocystoma
☐ C   rectal ulceration
☐ D   lymphoma
☐ E   neurofibromata

25. The ischiorectal fossae

- ☐ A   communicate across the midline
- ☐ B   contain the inferior rectal branches of the pudendal nerve
- ☐ C   have a base formed by skin
- ☐ D   have anterior recesses above the perineal membrane
- ☐ E   contain the internal pudendal vessels

26. Carcinoid syndrome

- ☐ A   generally produces paroxysmal flushing of the face and trunk
- ☐ B   flushing may be precipitated by alcohol
- ☐ C   has been shown to respond to octreotide
- ☐ D   does not respond to tumour debulking
- ☐ E   is associated with diarrhoea

27. Dermatomyositis

- ☐ A   is associated with ovarian carcinoma
- ☐ B   is associated with breast carcinoma
- ☐ C   is not known to precede the development of the neoplasm
- ☐ D   produces a characteristic urticarial rash around the eyelids
- ☐ E   improves with treatment of the underlying neoplasm

28. Fat embolism

- ☐ A   commonly occurs 3–4 days after a fracture
- ☐ B   can only be diagnosed by finding fat globules in either sputum or urine
- ☐ C   may present as an agitated patient
- ☐ D   is associated with hypoxia and hypercapnia
- ☐ E   is usually accompanied by a pyrexia

QUESTIONS – System Paper 4

67

29. **With bony metastatic disease the following statements are true:**

☐ A sclerotic metastases suggest a prostate primary
☐ B prophylactic internal fixation of a symptomatic deposit in a long bone should be considered
☐ C with a lung primary the prognosis is good
☐ D the primary tumour may be in the thyroid
☐ E treatment invariably involves chemotherapy

30. **Virchow's triad includes**

☐ A hypertension
☐ B endothelial damage
☐ C extrinsic vascular compression
☐ D altered blood constituents
☐ E hypoxaemia

31. **Abdominal aortic aneurysms (AAA)**

☐ A are four times more common in males
☐ B incidence is falling in Western countries
☐ C may be safely observed if asymptomatic and < 6 cm in size
☐ D has an operative mortality of 50% in cases of rupture
☐ E involves the suprarenal aorta in 10% of cases

32. **The radial artery**

☐ A anastomoses with the ulnar artery
☐ B passes over the trapezium in the wrist
☐ C passes into the hand between the two heads of the adductor pollicis muscle
☐ D lies lateral to the biceps tendon in the cubital fossa
☐ E is overlain by the pronator teres muscle

33. **The femoral artery**

❏ A underlies the inguinal ligament medial to the deep inguinal ring
❏ B supplies the hamstring muscles
❏ C supplies the head of the femur
❏ D passes through the adductor longus muscle
❏ E is subcutaneous in the femoral triangle

34. **The abdominal aorta**

❏ A enters the abdomen at the level of the T12 vertebra
❏ B divides at the level of the L5 vertebra
❏ C lies to the left of the cisterna chyli
❏ D gives off four single ventral gut arteries
❏ E lies posterior to the left renal vein

35. **In the popliteal fossa the**

❏ A roof is formed by the fascia lata
❏ B sciatic nerve divides into tibial and common peroneal branches
❏ C deepest structure is the popliteal vein
❏ D common peroneal nerve is overlain by the semitendinosus muscle
❏ E roof is pierced by sural nerve

36. **In the gluteal region, the sciatic nerve lies**

❏ A on the piriformis muscle
❏ B deep in the upper outer quadrant
❏ C on the capsule of the hip joint
❏ D medial to the inferior gluteal vessels
❏ E anterior to the obturator internus muscle

37. **Complications of carotid endarterectomy include**

- A   ipsilateral hypoglossal nerve injury
- B   ipsilateral glossopharyngeal nerve injury
- C   ipsilateral facial nerve injury
- D   stridor
- E   post-operative hypertension

38. **The biceps tendon reflex tests the integrity of**

- A   the musculocutaneous nerve
- B   the medial cord of the brachial plexus
- C   C5 spinal segment
- D   C6 dorsal root
- E   the middle trunk of the brachial plexus

39. **The triceps tendon reflex tests the integrity of the**

- A   lateral cord of the brachial plexus
- B   T1 ventral root
- C   C8 dorsal root
- D   upper trunk of the brachial plexus
- E   C7 spinal segment

40. **Avascular necrosis is a well recognised complication of**

- A   a fracture of the proximal pole of the scaphoid
- B   a supracondylar fracture of the distal humerus
- C   an inter-trochanteric fracture of the femoral neck
- D   a fracture of the talar neck
- E   a fracture of the hook of the hamate

41. **Oesophageal atresia**

- A   can occur without a tracheo-oesophageal fistula
- B   is frequently associated with other structural abnormalities
- C   definitive repair can be delayed for several months
- D   is associated with maternal polyhydramnios
- E   has an incidence of approximately 1:4000 live births

42. **Causes of acute respiratory distress in a 3-year-old male include**

❑ A   acute appendicitis
❑ B   crush injury to the abdomen
❑ C   congenital diaphragmatic hernia
❑ D   urinary tract infection
❑ E   inhaled foreign body

43. **In infantile hypertrophic pyloric stenosis**

❑ A   there is typically a hyperkalaemic, hyperchloraemic alkalosis
❑ B   the diagnosis is usually clinical
❑ C   the umbilicus should be avoided at operation
❑ D   females are more often affected
❑ E   jaundice is seen in 10% of children

44. **Congenital lymphoedema**

❑ A   may be treated by the Charles' operation
❑ B   is due to disease of superficial lymphatics
❑ C   may present after 30 years of age
❑ D   is more common in women
❑ E   is relieved by lymphovenous anastomosis

45. **The prostate gland**

❑ A   is pierced by the ducts of the seminal vesicles
❑ B   has a venous plexus contained within its capsule
❑ C   lies below the urogenital diaphragm
❑ D   contains the membranous urethra
❑ E   is separated from the rectum by peritoneum

46.   The base of the bladder lies on the

❑   A   seminal vesicles
❑   B   ureters
❑   C   ductus (vas) deferens
❑   D   anterior vaginal wall
❑   E   uterine cervix

47.   The posterior relations of the right kidney include the

❑   A   costodiaphragmatic space
❑   B   medial arcuate ligament
❑   C   sympathetic trunk
❑   D   iliohypogastric nerve
❑   E   11th rib

48.   Recognised causes of acute pancreatitis include

❑   A   calcium channel blockers
❑   B   mumps virus
❑   C   hypocalcaemia
❑   D   hyperlipidaemia
❑   E   polyarteritis nodosa

49.   Metastatic prostatic cancer

❑   A   is best treated with chemotherapy
❑   B   diethylstilboestrol therapy may be effective
❑   C   strontium may be used to reduce pain from widespread bone
          metastasis
❑   D   bicalutamide causes painful gynaecomastia
❑   E   LHRH analogues may cause distressing hot flushes

50. **A 64-year-old male presents with macroscopic haematuria. The following first-line investigations are indicated:**

❑ A MSU
❑ B urinary cytology
❑ C plain KUB X-ray
❑ D IVU
❑ E CT scan
❑ F cystogram
❑ G cystoscopy

51. **Pelvi-ureteric junction (PUJ) obstruction**

❑ A is more common in boys
❑ B is more common on the right
❑ C is best detected with a DMSA scan
❑ D when detected antenatally does not usually require in utero treatment

52. **The following stones form in acidic urine:**

❑ A cysteine
❑ B staghorn calculi
❑ C urate calculi
❑ D calcium phosphate
❑ E struvite calculi

SECTION 2 – EMQs

Theme: Hernias

A   Epigastric
B   Spigelian
C   Obturator
D   Lumbar
E   Gluteal
F   Sciatic hernia
G   Perineal hernia

For each site of herniation below, select the most likely hernial type from the list above. Each answer may be used once, more than once, or not at all.

- 61. Triangle of Petit
- 62. Greater sciatic notch
- 63. Pelvic floor
- 64. Linea semilunaris
- 65. Linea alba
- 66. Obturator canal
- 67. Lesser sciatic notch

Theme: Polyps

A   Tubular adenomatous polyps
B   Villous adenomatous polyps
C   Peutz–Jeghers polyps
D   Metaplastic polyps
E   Inflammatory polyps

For each of the descriptions below, select the most appropriate polyp from the list above. Each option may be used once, more than once, or not at all.

❏   68.   Are usually a consequence of a severe episode of ulcerative colitis
❏   69.   Are hamartomas
❏   70.   May cause hypokalaemia
❏   71.   Have the greatest malignant potential of all colonic polyps
❏   72.   Are the commonest type of polyp seen in familial adenomatous polyposis

Theme: Anatomy of the urogenital system

A   Uterus
B   Ligament of the ovary
C   Urethra
D   Bladder
E   Vas deferens
F   Suspensory ligament of the ovary
G   Testis
H   Perineal membrane

For each of the statements below, select the most likely option from the list above. Each option may be used once, more than once, or not at all.

❏   73.   Lies superior to the ureter
❏   74.   Transmits the ovarian vessels
❏   75.   Has an internal sphincter which contracts during ejaculation
❏   76.   Transmits the dorsal vein of the penis
❏   77.   Is separated from the rectum by peritoneum
❏   78.   Attaches the ovary to the uterus
❏   79.   Intervenes between the uterus and pubic symphysis

Theme: Knee Injuries

A   Injury to the medial meniscus
B   Anterior cruciate rupture
C   Patellar fracture
D   Haemarthrosis
E   Medial ligament rupture
F   Tibial plateau fracture

For each of the clinical situations described below, select the most likely diagnosis from the list above. Each option may be used once, more than once, or not at all.

80.   A 29-year-old man was hit by a car as he ran across the road to post a letter. He is unable to weight bear and the knee is bruised, swollen and tender.

81.   A 45-year-old lady stumbled over an uneven paving stone and landed heavily on her knee. She walked into casualty with help but has a swollen painful knee and is unable to straight leg raise.

82.   A footballer sustained a twisting injury to his weight bearing flexed knee whilst playing a game yesterday. He was unable to complete the game and by the morning his knee was very swollen. He was unable to fully flex or extend his knee.

83.   A 25-year-old man landed awkwardly having jumped for a ball in the lineout during an afternoon's rugby match. He heard a pop, and was unable to complete the game. He noticed that the knee became swollen immediately.

84.   A 25-year-old man was involved in a tackle during a football game today. A valgus force was applied to the knee – he fell to the ground and noted that his knee was at a 'funny angle'. He has been unable to weight bear and says that his knee feels 'unsafe'. On examination, the knee is generally tender, there is no definite effusion and significant laxity on varus/valgus stress.

QUESTIONS – System Paper 4

76

Theme: Site of arterial disease

A   Lower aorta
B   External iliac arteries
C   Common femoral arteries
D   Profunda femoral arteries
E   Left superficial femoral artery
F   Right internal iliac artery
G   Right peroneal artery
H   Right superficial femoral artery

For each of the clinical presentations below, select the most likely site of arterial disease from the list above. Each option may be used once, more than once, or not at all.

☐   85.   A heavy smoker presented with a history of buttock claudication and impotence
☐   86.   An elderly diabetic lady presented with gangrene of her right hallux

Theme: Anatomy of the pelvic vasculature

A   Superior gluteal artery
B   Superior vesical artery
C   Gonadal veins
D   Superior rectal vein
E   Inferior vesical artery
F   Lateral sacral veins
G   Internal iliac artery
H   Uterine artery

For each of the statements below, select the most likely option from the list above. Each option may be used once, more than once, or not at all.

☐   87.   Accompanies the ureter
☐   88.   Drains the middle third of the ureters
☐   89.   Is a branch of the posterior division of the internal iliac artery
☐   90.   Runs in the transverse cervical ligament (cardinal)
☐   91.   Communicates with the vertebral venous plexus
☐   92.   Forms the medial umbilical ligament
☐   93.   Supplies the prostate gland
☐   94.   Drains into the hepatic portal system

Theme: Benign prostatic hyperplasia

A   Doxazosin
B   Prazosin
C   TURP
D   Urethral catheterization
E   Retropubic (open) prostatectomy
F   Radical prostatectomy
G   Trial without catheter

For each of the patients below, select the most appropriate treatment from the list above. Each option may be used once, more than once or not at all.

❑   95.   A 71-year-old male presents with acute urinary retention. Upon catheterization his residual volume was 800 ml. His creatinine on admission was 350 µmol/l. Following management of a post-obstructive diuresis the creatinine returned to 90 µmol/l. Digital rectal examination suggested a large benign prostate. A transrectal ultrasound shows a prostate volume of 180 ml with no hypoechoic areas.

❑   96.   A 56-year-old male presents with moderate lower urinary tract symptoms. He has persistent macroscopic haematuria. A digital rectal examination showed a large benign feeling prostate. MSU, cytology, an IVU and flexible cystoscopy were negative for transitional cell carcinoma. He wishes to have another child in the near future.

❑   97.   A 59-year-old male presents with vague abdominal pain. An ultrasound showed bilateral hydronephrosis with a post-micturition residual volume of 1500 ml. His serum creatinine was normal.

Theme: Gastrointestinal haemorrhage

A   Colonoscopy
B   Oesophagoduodenoscopy
C   Selective mesenteric angiography
D   Red cell scan
E   Double contrast barium enema
F   Single contrast enema (Gastrografin)
G   Laparoscopy
H   CT colonography

For each of the patients described below, select the most appropriate investigation from the list above. Each option may be used once, more than once, or not at all.

❑   98.   A 45-year-old man is admitted to the Accident and Emergency Department with passage of large clots of fresh blood per rectum. There is no evidence of melaena. He is hypotensive with a blood pressure of 85/40 mmHg and a pulse of 140/min. There is no history of haematemesis but he is a smoker and drinks 20 units of alcohol per week.

❑   99.   An 85-year-old man is admitted with passage of dark clots per rectum. His blood pressure is 110/70 mmHg and his pulse is 90/min. He has been complaining recently of left-sided abdominal pain and change in bowel habit.

❑   100. A 25-year-old man attends the Outpatient Department with three episodes of bright red rectal bleeding. Rigid sigmoidoscopy and proctoscopy failed to reveal any local causes for the bleeding.

END OF SYSTEM PAPER 4

Time allowed: 2 hours
Indicate your answers in the spaces provided

SYSTEM PAPER 5
SECTION 1 – MCQS

1.   **Epistaxis**

   ❑   A   usually arises from the postero-medial nasal septum
   ❑   B   can be controlled by placement of a Fogarty balloon catheter
   ❑   C   may be a presentation of leukaemia
   ❑   D   may require ligation of the maxillary artery
   ❑   E   is best treated by bedrest and sedation

2.   **Parotid gland tumours**

   ❑   A   account for approximately 75% of all salivary gland tumours
   ❑   B   are most commonly benign
   ❑   C   are always slow growing
   ❑   D   can present with otalgia
   ❑   E   can be core biopsied safely with MRI

3.   **The submandibular gland**

   ❑   A   lies below the digastric muscle
   ❑   B   has the hyoglossal nerve running through it
   ❑   C   lies below and above the lower mandible
   ❑   D   is superficial to the hyoglossus
   ❑   E   has the facial artery running through it

4.   **An enlarging thyroid gland**

   ❑   A   extends into the chest anterior to the left brachiocephalic vein
   ❑   B   moves anterior to the internal jugular vein
   ❑   C   extends into the digastric triangle of the neck
   ❑   D   is enveloped by the prevertebral fascia
   ❑   E   moves on swallowing

5. **Transection of the cervical part of the sympathetic chain at the root of the neck results in**

☐ A vasomotor changes in the arm
☐ B ptosis
☐ C pupillary dilatation
☐ D ablation of sympathetic supply to the pulmonary plexus
☐ E loss of sweating over the C4 dermatome

6. **The middle meatus**

☐ A drains the naso-lacrimal duct
☐ B contains the bulla ethmoidalis
☐ C drains the sphenoidal air sinus
☐ D drains the posterior ethmoidal air sinus
☐ E is lined by olfactory epithelium

7. **Familial hypercalcaemic hypocalciuria**

☐ A may mimic primary hyperparathyroidism
☐ B is inherited in an autosomal recessive manner
☐ C does not produce elevated serum calcium levels
☐ D does not produce elevated parathyroid hormone levels
☐ E is associated with malignancy

8. **A Le Fort III maxillary fracture**

☐ A is usually treated conservatively
☐ B involves the lateral wall of the orbit
☐ C rarely results in malocclusion
☐ D may cause gross mid-facial swelling
☐ E involves the ethmoidal bone

9. **During a right hemicolectomy, the following structures are normally encountered during dissection:**

- ❏ A   caudate lobe
- ❏ B   inferior vena cava
- ❏ C   third part of the duodenum
- ❏ D   right ureter
- ❏ E   gonadal vessels

10. **Sigmoid volvulus**

- ❏ A   is seen most frequently in the sixth and seventh decades
- ❏ B   is a rare cause of colonic obstruction in Africa
- ❏ C   is associated with a long sigmoid mesenteric attachment
- ❏ D   usually twists in a clockwise direction
- ❏ E   is more common than caecal volvulus

11. **Faecal occult blood tests (guaiac based)**

- ❏ A   can detect blood loss of less than 0.5 ml/day
- ❏ B   rarely give rise to false positive results
- ❏ C   are unaffected by anatomical level of bleeding
- ❏ D   may be positive whilst taking oral iron
- ❏ E   is unaffected by faecal rehydration

12. **Causes of massive splenomegaly include**

- ❏ A   Chagas' disease
- ❏ B   malaria
- ❏ C   chronic hepatitis C
- ❏ D   chronic myeloid leukaemia
- ❏ E   myelofibrosis

13. **Glomus tumours**

- ❏ A   are derived from the Schwann cells
- ❏ B   only occur under the finger or toe nails
- ❏ C   typically give rise to paroxysms of severe pain
- ❏ D   have a malignant potential
- ❏ E   are typically palpable

14. **Investigations for carotid artery stenosis may include**

- [ ] A cervical plethysmography
- [ ] B duplex Doppler ultrasound
- [ ] C magnetic resonance angiography
- [ ] D selective internal carotid artery angiography
- [ ] E CT scan of the brain

15. **The posterior tibial artery**

- [ ] A is a branch of the popliteal artery
- [ ] B gives rise to the anterior tibial artery
- [ ] C gives rise to the peroneal artery
- [ ] D passes anterior to the fibrous arch of the soleus muscle
- [ ] E passes deep to the flexor retinaculum at the ankle

16. **The portal vein**

- [ ] A is formed behind the body of the pancreas
- [ ] B lies anteriorly in the free edge of the lesser omentum
- [ ] C drains the spleen
- [ ] D forms the central vein of each liver lobule
- [ ] E lies to the right of the superior mesenteric artery

17. **Stenosis of the superficial femoral artery**

- [ ] A is the commonest cause of intermittent claudication
- [ ] B can sometimes be dilated by angioplasty
- [ ] C may be associated with a fall in ankle pressure
- [ ] D can be bypassed
- [ ] E never results in gangrene

18. **Portal vein thrombosis may**

- [ ] A occur in patients with thrombophilia
- [ ] B occur after severe appendicitis
- [ ] C cause small bowel infarction
- [ ] D cause small intestinal varicosities
- [ ] E cause splenomegaly

19. **Compartment syndrome**

- ❏ A of the forearm commonly presents with pain on flexion of the fingers
- ❏ B commonly occurs with a Grade 3b open fracture of the tibia and fibula
- ❏ C is associated with an early reduction in the volume of the distal pulses
- ❏ D may occur following a soft tissue injury without a fracture
- ❏ E is diagnosed by a intra-compartmental pressure reading within 30 mmHg of the systolic blood pressure

20. **Varicose veins**

- ❏ A are usually due to superficial femoral vein reflux
- ❏ B may cause leg ulcers
- ❏ C may thrombose
- ❏ D cause increased venous pressure on exercise
- ❏ E can be treated with 10% ethanolamine

21. **Complications of laparoscopic surgery include**

- ❏ A surgical emphysema
- ❏ B nitric oxide embolus
- ❏ C pneumothorax
- ❏ D trocar injuries to the iliac artery
- ❏ E laser injury

22. **The following patients should be considered for screening for colorectal carcinoma:**

- ❏ A the brother of a patient with familial adenomatous polyposis
- ❏ B a patient with long-standing ulcerative colitis
- ❏ C a patient with long-standing Peutz–Jeghers syndrome
- ❏ D a patient with Gardner's syndrome
- ❏ E a patient with long-standing diverticular disease

23.   In surgery for Crohn's disease

☐   A   bowel should be resected back to microscopically normal bowel to prevent recurrence

☐   B   in the presence of several short segment small bowel strictures, multiple small resections are preferred to multiple stricturoplasties

☐   C   if proctocolectomy is indicated, rectal excision should preserve perirectal tissues

☐   D   perianal abscesses in Crohn's disease are managed with antibiotics

24.   Colon cancer

☐   A   is the commonest cause of death due to malignancy in the UK

☐   B   has a slight female predominance

☐   C   has a male predominance

☐   D   has an equal incidence in developed and underdeveloped countries

☐   E   has an increasing relative incidence in the right colon in developed countries

25.   In the inguinal region

☐   A   the pectineal ligament is otherwise known as Astley Cooper's ligament

☐   B   the lacunar ligament is otherwise known as Poupart's ligament

☐   C   the inguinal ligament is otherwise known as Gimbernat's ligament

☐   D   the transversalis fascia is otherwise known as Scarpa's fascia

☐   E   Cloquet's node lies within the femoral canal

26.   Early poor prognostic factors for acute pancreatitis include

☐   A   a serum amylase of > 2000 i.u.

☐   B   a blood glucose level of > 6 mmol/l

☐   C   a serum calcium of < 2.4 mmol/l

☐   D   WCC > 15 x 10^9/l

☐   E   pO$_2$ < 8 kPa

☐   F   blood urea > 10 mmol/l despite adequate fluid replacement

☐   G   haemoglobin < 10 g/dl

27. **Ultrasound findings in acute cholecystitis may include**

❏ A   gall bladder calculi with posterior acoustic enhancement
❏ B   biliary sludge
❏ C   pericholecystic fluid
❏ D   oedema of the pancreatic head
❏ E   common bile duct dilatation in 10% of cases
❏ F   cystic duct dilatation

28. **Femoral hernia**

❏ A   has a high risk of strangulation
❏ B   is easily missed in the obese
❏ C   is equally common in males and females
❏ D   has a neck lying at the level of the inguinal ligament
❏ E   may be revealed by scrotal skin invagination

29. **In gallstone disease**

❏ A   approximately 50% of patients are symptomatic
❏ B   the pain of biliary colic is due to gall bladder ischaemia
         resulting from temporary cystic duct obstruction
❏ C   a mucocele of the gall bladder characteristically contains
         infected bile
❏ D   acute cholecystitis is often associated with gall bladder
         mucosal ulceration
❏ E   an empyema of the gall bladder may cause septic shock
❏ F   acute cholecystitis infrequently perforates

30. **Solitary rectal ulcer syndrome**

❏ A   usually produces bright red rectal bleeding
❏ B   is associated with excessive passage of mucus
❏ C   symptoms are due to repeated anal dilatation
❏ D   rectal biopsies show pallisading basal cells
❏ E   is best treated by excision of the ulcer

31. **Indications for surgery in ulcerative colitis include**

- [ ] A failure of a significant response to medical treatment of a severe flare after 48 hours
- [ ] B acute toxic megacolon
- [ ] C failure of adequate medical treatment of chronic disease over a prolonged period of time
- [ ] D the presence of confirmed mild dysplasia on colonic biopsies
- [ ] E total colitis

32. **The third part of the duodenum lies**

- [ ] A posterior to the superior mesenteric vessels
- [ ] B immediately anterior to the right renal artery
- [ ] C posterior to the root of the mesentery of the small bowel
- [ ] D anterior to the right ureter
- [ ] E anterior to the inferior mesenteric artery

33. **The kidneys**

- [ ] A initially develop at the level of the L1 vertebra
- [ ] B have hila in the transpyloric plane
- [ ] C are palpable in the hypochondrial areas
- [ ] D are both covered by the pancreas
- [ ] E lie on the lateral arcuate ligaments

34. **The superficial inguinal lymph nodes drain the**

- [ ] A skin of the gluteal region
- [ ] B skin of the peri-anal region
- [ ] C uterus
- [ ] D testis
- [ ] E skin of the dorsum of the foot

35.   In the inguinal canal the

☐ A   inferior epigastric artery lies lateral to the internal ring
☐ B   lacunar ligament forms part of the floor
☐ C   transversalis fascia forms the posterior wall throughout
☐ D   roof is formed by the transversus abdominis muscle
☐ E   ilioinguinal nerve enters through the internal ring

36.   The obturator nerve

☐ A   arises from the L2–4 roots
☐ B   lies above the obturator vessels
☐ C   has no cutaneous branches
☐ D   receives its parasympathetic fibres from sacral segments of the cord
☐ E   supplies the knee joint

37.   Osteosarcoma

☐ A   must be considered if an osteochondroma suddenly increases in size in adulthood
☐ B   commonly presents in the second and third decades
☐ C   commonly affects the diaphysis of growing bones
☐ D   is usually treated by amputation
☐ E   may complicate Paget's disease

38.   Common early signs of suppurative tenosynovitis of the flexor tendons of the hand include

☐ A   the affected finger held in full flexion
☐ B   a swinging pyrexia
☐ C   pain on passive finger movement
☐ D   fusiform swelling of the finger
☐ E   tenderness of the palm

39. A deep laceration into the thenar eminence could damage the

❏ A superficial palmar arterial arch
❏ B muscular recurrent branch of the median nerve
❏ C radial artery
❏ D flexor digitorum superficialis tendons
❏ E adductor pollicis muscle

40. Fracture of the lower end of the ulna

❏ A classically occurs after falling on the outstretched hand
❏ B impairs pronation
❏ C impairs adduction of the wrist
❏ D impairs movements of the little finger
❏ E involves the wrist joint

41. At the ankle joint the

❏ A peroneus tertius tendon grooves the lateral malleolus
❏ B flexor digitorum longus tendon grooves the medial malleolus
❏ C deltoid ligament is attached to the calcaneus
❏ D posterior tibial artery lies between the tibialis posterior and flexor digitorum longus tendons
❏ E tibial nerve lies anterior to the posterior tibial artery

42. Complications of a supracondylar fracture of the humerus in a child include

❏ A compartment syndrome
❏ B growth arrest
❏ C cubitus valgus
❏ D anterior interosseus nerve palsy
❏ E brachial artery spasm

43. **Congenital diaphragmatic hernia**

☐ A   is found on the left side in over 75% of cases
☐ B   can be detected on prenatal ultrasound scanning
☐ C   should be regarded as a surgical emergency and be repaired immediately
☐ D   may present late with failure to thrive
☐ E   is associated with gut malrotation

44. **Meckel's diverticulum**

☐ A   is a common cause of rectal bleeding in children
☐ B   is an embryological remnant of the vitello-intestinal duct
☐ C   can contain ectopic appendiceal mucosa
☐ D   when found in an inguinal hernia is known as a Littre's hernia
☐ E   can be localised by an MIBG scan when it contains ectopic acid secreting mucosa

45. **Duodenal atresia**

☐ A   is associated with trisomy 21
☐ B   is corrected by a gastro-enterostomy
☐ C   is not usually obvious on plain AXR
☐ D   can present at six weeks of age

46. **Infantile hypertrophic pyloric stenosis**

☐ A   has an approximate incidence of 3:1000 live births
☐ B   is associated with bile stained vomiting
☐ C   has no known familial association
☐ D   does not occur in premature babies
☐ E   requires a 'test feed' to palpate the classical 'olive'

47.   **Intussusception**

❑   A   is the commonest cause of small bowel obstruction under the age of 18 months
❑   B   classically presents with 'brick red' coloured stool
❑   C   is infrequently associated with a pathological 'lead-point' over the age of 18 months
❑   D   can be treated safely with an air enema
❑   E   is an unusual cause of unexplained collapse in a child

48.   **Concerning treatment of organ-confined prostate cancer**

❑   A   if treated conservatively has an 85% disease specific survival at 10 years
❑   B   radical prostatectomy is associated with a 15% complete incontinence rate
❑   C   radical prostatectomy may be performed through a perineal or retropubic approach
❑   D   cryotherapy is a widely accepted treatment option
❑   E   brachytherapy implies the implantation of radioactive seeds within the prostate

49.   **Carcinoma of the penis**

❑   A   is common in under-developed countries
❑   B   is rare in males circumcised at birth
❑   C   can be treated with brachytherapy
❑   D   is associated with Bouin's disease
❑   E   almost always has a poor prognosis when presenting with palpable inguinal nodes

50.   **Neuropathic bladder dysfunction is associated with**

❑   A   spina bifida
❑   B   diabetes mellitus
❑   C   abdominal hysterectomy
❑   D   anterior resection
❑   E   vesico-ureteric reflux

51.   Urinary incontinence

❏   A   may be secondary to urinary retention
❏   B   following TURP almost always implies iatrogenic damage to
            the external urinary sphincter
❏   C   in females may be treated with a prolene tape slung around
            the mid-urethra
❏   D   complete incontinence is seen in approximately 3% of cases
            following radical prostatectomy
❏   E   can be treated by pelvic floor exercises if due to stress
            incontinence

**52.   A 42-year-old male presents with severe colicky pain in his
            left loin radiating to his left testis. His temperature is normal.
            Dipstix testing reveals microscopic haematuria. An IVU
            shows a 4 mm stone in the lower third of the ureter causing
            partial obstruction. Which of the following treatment options
            applies:**

❏   A   a period of conservative management is advised
❏   B   ureteroscopy if conservative management fails
❏   C   ESWL if conservative management fails
❏   D   percutaneous nephrostomy and insertion of antegrade stent if
            conservative management fails
❏   E   high intensity focused ultrasound (HIFU) if conservative
            management fails

SECTION 2 – EMQs

Theme: Medical therapy for surgical conditions

A   Hypercalcaemia
B   Carcinoid syndrome
C   Resistant Crohn's disease
D   Disseminated prostatic cancer
E   Breast cancer
F   Thyrotoxicosis

For each of the drugs listed below, select the most appropriate condition from the list above. Each option may be used once, more than once, or not at all.

- 61. Azathioprine
- 62. Anastrozole
- 63. Mithramycin
- 64. Carbimazole
- 65. Flutamide
- 66. Streptozotocin

Theme: Hernias

A   Richter's hernia
B   Littre's hernia
C   Maydl's hernia
D   Sliding hernia
E   Pantaloon hernia

For each description listed below, select the most appropriate hernia from the list above. Each option may be used once, more than once, or not at all.

- 67. Dual sacs straddling the inferior epigastric vessels
- 68. Two separate loops of bowel
- 69. The posterior wall of the hernial sac is formed by a herniating viscus
- 70. Portion of circumference of the bowel
- 71. Meckel's diverticulum

Theme: Jaundice

A   Pre-hepatic jaundice
B   Hepatic jaundice
C   Post-hepatic jaundice

For each of the conditions below, select the most likely type of jaundice they would be associated with from the list above. Each option may be used once, more than once, or not at all.

- [ ] 72. Chlorpromazine induced jaundice
- [ ] 73. Chronic active hepatitis
- [ ] 74. Halothane induced jaundice
- [ ] 75. Thalassaemia
- [ ] 76. Sclerosing cholangitis
- [ ] 77. Hepatic abscesses
- [ ] 78. Rotor's syndrome

Theme: Infective and non-infective intestinal inflammation

A   Amoebic dysentery
B   Yersinia enterocolitis
C   Pseudomembranous colitis
D   Infective colitis
E   Diversion colitis

For each of the statements below, select the most likely form of intestinal inflammation from the list above. Each option may be used once, more than once, or not at all.

- [ ] 79. Is associated with an acute ileitis and inflamed mesenteric lymph nodes
- [ ] 80. The main histological features are oedema of the lamina propria and a predominantly polymorphonuclear infiltrate
- [ ] 81. Is postulated to be due to a local butyrate deficiency
- [ ] 82. Is typically associated with flask-shaped ulcers
- [ ] 83. Is associated with characteristic yellow plaques on sigmoidoscopy

Theme: Paediatric investigations

A   A 'Double Bubble' on plain AXR
B   A 'cone' on contrast enema
C   A hypochloraemic metabolic alkalosis
D   Intra-mural gas on plain AXR
E   Air filled cysts in the left chest
F   A 'Target' lesion on abdominal ultrasound
G   A type II curve on a diuretic renogram
H   Clubbed renal calyces on a micturating cystogram

For each of the clinical scenarios below, select the most appropriate feature on investigation from the list above. Each option may be used once, more than once, or not at all.

❏   84.   A 10-hour-old term female with persistent non-bile stained vomiting
❏   85.   A 10-day-old baby, born at 31 weeks, with bile stained vomiting and bleeding per rectum
❏   86.   An 8-month-old infant with colicky abdominal pain and bleeding PR
❏   87.   A 2-day-old baby with abdominal distension, bile stained vomiting and failure to pass meconium

Theme: Peripheral nerve anatomy

A   Saphenous
B   Femoral
C   Obturator
D   Sural
E   Common peroneal
F   Tibial
G   Sciatic
H   Medial cutaneous nerve of the thigh

For each of the clinical scenarios below, select the nerve most likely to be involved from the list above. Each option may be used once, more than once, or not at all.

88. After removal of a below knee plaster cast, applied for an Achilles' tendon avulsion, a 16-year-old boy notices that the side of his leg and top of his foot is numb and that he frequently trips while walking, particularly when climbing stairs.

89. A 35-year-old lady, who was subsequently found to have a large left-sided cystic ovarian tumour, presents with pain radiating down the medial part of the thigh and a 'bearing down' feeling in her pelvis.

90. A 25-year-old female suddenly experiences severe pain in her back with shooting pains passing down the back of her left calf into the lateral part of the left foot. X-ray shows a prolapsed disc on the left between L5 and S1. The only neurological finding on examination is loss of discriminatory touch over the area of painful skin.

91. An 18-year-old motorcyclist is involved in a RTA and sustains a fracture dislocation of the right hip. The painful thigh is difficult to examine, but there is an obvious foot drop and sensory loss below the knee except in skin on the medial part of the leg and foot and upper posterior part of the calf.

Theme: Anatomy of the posterior abdominal wall

A   Kidney
B   Psoas major muscle
C   Lumbar plexus
D   Ureter
E   Sympathetic trunk
F   Ilioinguinal nerve
G   Bare area of the liver
H   Superior rectal artery

For each of the statements below, select the most likely option from the list above. Each option may be used once, more than once, or not at all.

92. Tracts pus to the femoral triangle
93. Lies in the root of the sigmoid mesentery
94. Lies behind the aorta
95. Lies behind the kidney
96. Lies medial to the left ureter
97. Is embedded in the psoas major muscle
98. Lies anterior to the subcostal vessels
99. Contacts the right suprarenal gland

Theme: Testicular tumours

A   Close follow-up
B   Testicular biopsy
C   Anti-androgen therapy
D   Radiotherapy
E   Chemotherapy
F   Radical orchidectomy
G   Retroperitoneal lymph node dissection

For each of the patients below, select the most appropriate subsequent treatment from the list above. Each option may be used once, more than once, or not at all.

☐   100. A 34-year-old man presents with a hard irregular swelling of his right testis. α-fetoprotein and β hCG are normal. An ultrasound shows a heterogenous mass in the upper pole of the right testis. A radical orchidectomy confirms a testicular seminoma which is completely excised.

☐   101. A 22-year-old male presents with a hard, irregular swelling of his right testis. Ultrasound suggests a right testicular tumour and a left testis containing hypoechoic areas and microcalcification. A right radical orchidectomy and a left testicular biopsy are performed. Histology shows the right testicular seminoma is completely excised. On the left widespread intra-tubular germ cell neoplasia is found.

☐   102. A 24-year-old male underwent an orchidectomy for a non-seminatous germ cell tumour. A post-operative CT scan shows a 7 cm mass of retroperitoneal lymphadenopathy. After a course of chemotherapy his tumour markers normalise and CT scanning shows shrinkage of the nodal mass to 3.5 cm.

END OF SYSTEM PAPER 5

1.   Follicular carcinoma of the thyroid   Answer: D
Follicular carcinoma of the thyroid accounts for approximately 30% of differentiated thyroid cancers. Follicular carcinoma is found mainly in low-iodine intake areas, is solitary, encapsulated, invades veins and spreads to bones. The treatment for follicular carcinoma is total thyroidectomy as it allows subsequent treatment with radio-iodine. Prognosis is better in patients between 20 and 50 years. Children have an overall poorer prognosis.

2.   Papillary carcinoma of the thyroid   Answer: C
Papillary thyroid carcinoma is more common in females (4:1), and has a median age of onset at 20–30 years. It arises from parenchymal follicular cells. High dietary iodine intake increases the incidence of papillary carcinoma. Low iodine is goitrogenic and may lead to development of follicular and anaplastic carcinoma. Medullary thyroid carcinoma is associated with MEN IIA and IIB in 30% of cases.

3.   Salivary gland calculi   Answers: C D
Salivary gland calculi are most commonly found in the submandibular gland (80% cases) and are associated with a high pH and higher mucus content. They most commonly occur in the fourth and fifth decades. Calculi are associated with chronic sialadenitis, diabetes mellitus, hypertension and chronic liver disease. Only 20% of submandibular and 60% of parotid stones are visible on X-ray.

4.   Midline swellings of the neck   Answers: B C
Swellings of the neck considered to be midline include thyroglossal cysts, (pharyngeal pouches,) plunging ranulas, subhyoid bursas, laryngocoeles, and lesions in the thyroid isthmus.

5.   The parotid gland   Answers: A B D
The fibrous capsule of the parotid gland is an upward extension of the deep investing layer of cervical fascia which attaches to the zygomatic arch. The medial wall of the capsule is separated from the carotid sheath by the styloid process and associated muscles. The external carotid artery passes through the gland supplying it as it does so. No facial vessels are related to the gland.

6.   Arterial clips   Answers: A C

When ligating the inferior thyroid arteries, the recurrent laryngeal nerves are vulnerable. When ligating the superior thyroid arteries, the external laryngeal nerves running alongside may be damaged. The internal laryngeal nerves pass above and behind the root of the superior thyroid arteries and are thus usually outside the operative field. The phrenic nerves are protected behind the prevertebral fascia. Both transverse cervical nerves run in the subcutaneous fascia, horizontal skin crease thyroidectomy incisions run parallel with their course and thus most branches of these cutaneous nerves are spared.

7.   Resection of terminal ileum   Answers: B E

The terminal ileum is the primary site for absorption of the fat soluble vitamins B_{12} and K. In addition, bile salts are predominantly absorbed here. Calcium and folic acid are predominantly absorbed, more proximally, in the jejunum.

8.   Blood film post-splenectomy   Answers: A C D

One of the functions of the spleen is sequestration and phagocytosis of old or abnormal red cells. Therefore, in a post-splenectomy patient, red cell inclusion bodies may be present producing target cells, Howell-Jolly bodies and sideroblasts. Punctate basophilia is seen in patients with lead poisoning, thalassaemia and haemolytic anaemias due to pyrimidine-5-nucleotidase deficiency. Rouleaux is the tendency of red cells to stack up like a pile of coins. The amount of rouleaux formation is determined by the concentration of protein in the plasma.

9.   Squamous cell carcinoma of anal canal   Answers: A B

Rectal bleeding is the most common initial symptom (45% cases). 30% complain of pain or sensation of a mass. The human papilloma virus (usually Type 16) may cause intra-epithelial neoplasia, which with time progresses to anal carcinoma. This virus is found in approximately 70% of patients. Other risk factors for anal carcinoma include a history of cervical or vaginal cancer, history of sexual transmitted disease and immunosuppression after solid organ transplantation. Lymphatic drainage – above the dentate line flows to the peri-rectal and para-vertebral nodes; below the dentate line, drainage is through the inguinal and femoral nodes. Anal carcinoma is relatively radio-sensitive. Presently, combination radiotherapy and chemotherapy (5 FU ± mitomycin or 5 FU and cisplatin) is used as initial standard, first-line treatment. Abdomino-perineal resection is reserved for recurrent or resistant tumours.

10. Patients with jaundice   Answers: C E

Urobilinogen in the urine suggests a pre-hepatic cause, and bilirubin in the urine suggests a post-hepatic cause. Elevated serum alkaline phosphatase is usually indicative of post-hepatic disease e.g. stone in the common bile duct or pancreatic carcinoma. A raised gamma glutamyl transferase may indicate a hepatic cause but is non-specifically elevated when any insult is placed on the liver.

11. Indications for ERCP   Answers: D E

ERCP can be both diagnostic and therapeutic. It can be used to examine both the biliary tree and pancreatic duct. Biliary strictures and bile duct calculi can be identified. Sphincterotomy can be performed for intraductal biliary calculi and stents can be inserted to assist bile drainage as in malignant obstruction.

12. Gardner's syndrome   Answers: A D

Extra-intestinal manifestations of Gardner's syndrome include osteomas (especially of the skull and mandible) mesenteric and abdominal wall desmoids, lipomas, fibromas, and epidermoid cysts. It is probably part of the same spectrum of disease to which FAP belongs, but has more prominent extraintestinal manifestations.

13. Choledocholithiasis   Answer: A

10–15% of patients with acute cholecystitis will have CBD calculi. CBD stones of less than a few millimetres will usually pass spontaneously into the duodenum without complication, but larger stones usually require manual extraction. Intra-operative cholangiography misses CBD stones in 5% of cases. ERCP stone extraction usually requires sphincterotomy. Liver function tests improve following surgical removal of calculi if there is no residual duct obstruction.

14. Meckel's diverticulum   Answers: All false

A Meckel's diverticulum occurs in approximately 2% of people, and though its precise location varies, it is usually about two feet proximal to the ileocaecal valve. It may contain ectopic, gastric, duodenal or pancreatic tissue, all of which may lead to GI haemorrhage. Meckel's diverticulum is usually uncomplicated at diagnosis, but can become acutely inflamed, perforate, bleed, herniate, or cause obstruction. A Meckel's diverticulum may be seen on a red cell scan when associated with bleeding.

15.   Pseudomembranous colitis   Answers: A C E
Pseudomembranous colitis (PMC) has been reported to occur following the use of a wide range of antibiotics. A single dose of antibiotic may be enough to cause PMC. The clinical effects are due to *Clostridium difficile* toxin, which may be isolated in the stool in over 90% of affected patients. *Clostridium difficile* itself is difficult to culture under normal circumstances. Typically, yellow plaques form on the mucosal surface, and are comprised of epithelial debris, mucin, fibrin, and polymorphs. The treatment of choice is oral metronidazole or vancomycin. The condition uncommonly progresses to toxic megacolon and perforation.

16.   Inflammatory bowel disease   Answers: B C E F
Ocular extra-intestinal manifestations of inflammatory bowel disease include episcleritis and uveitis. Cutaneous manifestations include erythema nodosum and pyoderma gangrenosum. 75% of patients with primary sclerosing cholangitis have underlying ulcerative colitis. Sclerosing cholangitis occurs rarely with Crohn's disease. Hepatic cirrhosis occurs in 1–5% of patients with ulcerative colitis, and only rarely with Crohn's. Other hepatobiliary manifestations include mild abnormalities of liver function tests, fatty liver, pericholangitis, and bile duct carcinoma. Ankylosing spondylitis occurs in 5% of cases of IBD. Arthritis (large joint) is the most common extra-intestinal manifestation of IBD. Urinary calculi form in up to 10% of IBD patients, especially those with an ileostomy.

17.   Crohn's disease   Answer: D
Smoking appears protective against ulcerative colitis, but increases the risk of developing Crohn's disease and doubles the risk of post-operative recurrence. There is some evidence that measles virus may have a causal relationship with Crohn's disease, but no definitive link has been established. When considering the extended family, 20–30% of patients with Crohn's disease have a positive family history. The risk of a child of a patient with Crohn's disease developing the disease is approximately 2%.

18.   Ulcerative colitis   Answers: C E
Abdominal signs may be masked by steroids. Toxic dilatation is more common in ulcerative colitis than in Crohn's disease. Sequential AXR monitors are an important means of patient monitoring for the development of toxic dilatation and perforation in patients with total severe colitis. Only in sick patients with severe colitis does a colonic diameter of > 6.5 cm indicate toxic megacolon. A diameter of this size in a well patient without abdominal signs is unlikely to be due to toxic dilatation. In severe ulcerative colitis, the haemoglobin ↓, the WBC ↑, Albumin ↓ and both the ESR ↑ and CRP ↑.

19.   Entero-vesical fistulae   **Answers: A B**

About 50% of entero-vesical fistulae are secondary to diverticular disease, 15–20% are secondary to colorectal cancer, 15–20% are secondary to Crohn's disease, and about 5% are secondary to bladder tumours. About 60% of patients have pneumaturia, and 30% have faecaluria.

20.   Pancreatic carcinoma   **Answers: A B C**

Pancreatic carcinoma is more common in men and rarely develops before the age of 50 years. Cigarette smoking is 2–3 times more common in pancreatic carcinoma. A large case control study has correlated chronic pancreatitis with increased risk of pancreatic cancer. More than 90% of pancreatic cancers are ductal adenocarcinomas. Pain and weight loss are present in more than 75% of patients. Infrequent presentations include: glucose intolerance, palpable gall bladder, migratory thrombophlebitis and splenomegaly.

21.   Abdominal aortic aneurysm   **Answers: A B D**

An abdominal aneurysm may rupture or cause embolization. They can be identified by screening programmes and there is current interest in endovascular stenting. Presently, only certain configurations of AAA can be successfully stented. Extension of the aneurysm above the renal arteries precludes stenting. Current practice is to defer operative intervention until the maximum diameter is at least 5.5 cm. The UK small aneurysm trial (1998) reported no survival benefit for early operation in patients with small (4.0 to 5.5 cm) aortic aneurysms. However, clinical decision making should be strongly guided by patient preferences and explanation of the risks of surgery.

22.   Vascular lesions of the skin   **Answers: A B D**

Naevus flammeus (salmon patch) is the common birthmark, and appears as a flat pink, red or purple patch, most commonly on the face and neck of newborns. Most involute by one year. Port wine stains are a variant of naevus flammeus, but these lesions grow with the child, becoming elevated and unsightly. They show little or no tendency to regress with time. Spider naevi comprise a small cutaneous arteriole from which small venules radiate. They are common in pregnancy and liver failure. Juvenile haemangiomas usually undergo a rapid growth phase over several months to produce the protruding strawberry naevus. They subsequently regress, and most involute to a small brown spot by the age of seven years. Cavernous haemangiomas tend to grow with time and rarely involute.

23. Critical leg ischaemia   Answers: B D

Critical leg ischaemia is defined by either of the two following criteria:

- Persistently recurring rest pain requiring regular, adequate analgesia for more than two weeks with an ankle systolic pressure of less than 50 mmHg and/or a toe systolic pressure of less than 30 mmHg.
- Ulceration or gangrene of the foot or toes with an ankle systolic pressure of less than 50 mmHg and/or a toe systolic pressure of less than 30 mmHg

Critically ischaemic legs due to distal occlusion or embolization may be treated with thrombolysis (using streptokinase or tissue plasminogen activator). However, thrombolysis may take several hours to take effect and a clinical decision has to be made regarding whether one can wait this length of time before an irreversible situation is reached. Lumbar sympathectomy may help patients with mild rest pain. It is, however, ineffective once frank gangrene is present.

24. The external inguinal ring   Answers: B C E G

The external inguinal ring is formed by a V slit in the external oblique aponeurosis. It transmits the testicular artery (a branch of the aorta on the right and of the renal artery on the left), the cremasteric artery (a branch of the inferior epigastric artery), the genital branch of the genito-femoral nerve, the pampiniform plexus, the ilioinguinal nerve, and the cremasteric muscle.

25. Femoral region   Answers: A C D

The femoral sheath contains the femoral artery and vein. The femoral canal lies medial to the femoral vein, between its medial border and the femoral sheath. The femoral canal contains the lymph node of Cloquet. The femoral ring is the abdominal end of the femoral canal. The pubic branch of the inferior epigastric artery replaces the obturator artery in 30% of cases, and may be at risk in a femoral hernia repair.

26. The orbit   Answers: A B C

The optic nerve and retina are part of the CNS. The optic nerve is invested by all meningeal layers. Since the central retinal artery travels in the optic nerve after branching off the ophthalmic artery, damage to the optic nerve commonly causes retinal infarction. Ptosis is a feature of both IIIrd nerve lesions and Horner's syndrome. The afferent arc of the corneal reflex is the nasociliary branch of Va. Blow out fractures of the orbit either detach the suspensory ligament of the eye, or entrap the recti muscles, usually the inferior rectus muscle; both conditions are associated with diplopia.

27. The brachial artery
Answers: A B D E

The brachial pulse is felt in the cubital fossa medial to the biceps tendon. In the arm, the ulnar nerve lies posterior proximally but, more distally, it leaves the artery after piercing the medial intermuscular septum. The artery is surrounded by venae comitantes, reinforced by the basilic vein which perforates the deep fascia opposite the deltoid tubercle, and is crossed anteriorly by the median nerve in the middle of the arm which lies lateral, above, and medial, below. In the cubital fossa, the artery is overlain by the bicipital aponeurosis.

28. The carpal tunnel
Answers: A E

The carpal tunnel contains the median nerve, the flexor carpi radialis, flexor pollicis longus, and flexor digitalis superficialis and brevis tendons. The ulnar artery and nerve, and the flexor carpi ulnaris tendon lie outside the tunnel.

29. The greater sciatic foramen
Answers: A B C E

The greater sciatic notch is converted into the greater sciatic foramen by the sacrospinous ligament, and transmits many structures including the superior gluteal nerve above, and the pudendal and posterior cutaneous femoral nerves below the piriformis muscle. The tendon of the obturator internus muscle passes through the lesser sciatic foramen.

30. The femoral triangle
Answers: A D E

The superficial epigastric and superficial external pudendal arteries pass through the saphenous opening (the superficial circumflex and deep external pudendal arteries pierce the fascia lata). The femoral artery separates the femoral nerve (laterally) from the femoral vein (medially). The profunda femoris artery is a lateral branch of the femoral artery. The deep inguinal nodes lie medial to the femoral vein. The femoral sheath encloses the femoral vessels for some 3 cm beyond the inguinal ligament, where the sheath terminates by fusing with the adventitia of both vessels.

31. Typical thoracic vertebra
Answers: A C D E

The four demi-facets articulate with a rib above and below on each side. The tubercles of the ribs articulating with the upper demi-facets articulate with a facet on the transverse processes of this same vertebra. Only rotation is possible between thoracic vertebrae (flexion and extension of the spine is a function of lumbar vertebrae); the movement occurs at the secondary cartilaginous intervertebral joints.

32.   The appendix   Answers: All false
The appendix opens on the posteromedial wall of the caecum, lies lateral to the right ureter and right gonadal vessels, and has a continuous longitudinal muscular coat. The mesoappendix carries the appendicular artery. Two small folds of peritoneum should not be confused with the mesoappendix. One extends from the front of the mesoappendix to the ileum, the ileocaecal fold (bloodless fold of Treves), and the other from the terminal part of the root of the small bowel mesentery to the anterior wall of the caecum, the vascular fold of the caecum, containing the anterior caecal artery.

33.   The left ureter   Answers: B C
The left ureter lies under the peritoneum behind the left colic and gonadal vessels, but anterior to the genito-femoral nerve. It crosses the pelvic brim over the bifurcation of the common iliac vessels in the apex of the sigmoid mesocolon. Before entering the bladder, it passes underneath the vas (water under the bridge).

34.   The spleen   Answers: A C E
The spleen lies on the diaphragm, separated from the 9th – 11th ribs by the costodiaphragmatic space. The left extremity of the lesser sac extends into the hilum. The peritoneal fold of the lienorenal ligament (which contains the tail of the pancreas touching the spleen) passes from the left kidney to the spleen. The spleen is not palpable in the healthy individual, and must at least double in size before it appears in the left hypochondrium along the line of the 10th rib.

35.   The female reproductive tract   Answers: A C D E
Most of the anterior surface of the uterus is applied to the posterior surface of the bladder. Ureteric calculi are palpable through the posterior fornix, lateral to the cervix where the ureter passes under the uterine artery (water under the bridge). Lymphatic drainage of the medial part of the Fallopian tubes and uterine fundus is via lymphatics in the broad ligament to the superficial inguinal nodes.

36.   The rectum   Answers: A D
The upper two-thirds of the rectum is retroperitoneal, the lower third is opposed to the bladder in the male and the vagina in the female. Its lymphatic drainage is upwards via nodes along the inferior mesenteric artery and pre-aortic nodes.

37.   The anal canal   **Answers: A C D E**

The levator ani form part of the deep external anal sphincter. The anal canal has no longitudinal muscular coat. The entire anal sphincter is innervated by the inferior rectal branch of the pudendal nerve. Lymph from the lower anal canal drains via the superficial inguinal nodes. The valves of the anal canal are formed by horizontal folds of mucous membrane between adjacent columns.

38.   Internal fixation of fractures   **Answers: A B D E**

Open fractures are more appropriately treated by external fixation, but if a closed fracture is converted to an open fracture in order to deal with a soft tissue or vascular injury then internal fixation is advised. Similarly, failure to obtain or maintain a satisfactory reduction of a fracture by closed means dictates that an open reduction be considered. This is followed by internal fixation if appropriate. Pathological fractures are likely to heal slowly (if at all) and thus internal fixation methods allow prompt mobilisation.

39.   Compound fracture   **Answers: B D E**

The principles of management of a compound fracture include a full assessment of the patient and thus the ABC's of trauma must be included and assessment against the GCS is appropriate. Management should also include parenteral antibiotics, antiseptic dressing, analgesia, anti-tetanus treatment and alignment of the limb with immobilisation. (The 5As.) A plaster cast will not immobilise a proximal femoral fracture – traction would be more appropriate.

40.   Testicular torsion   **Answers: B D**

This condition occurs in young men and the patient presents with sudden pain and an extremely tender testicle. It is commoner in patients with incompletely descended testes and can be imitated by a torsion of the hydatid of Morgagni. The diagnosis can be confirmed by Duplex scanning but this is not reliable. Immediate exploration should be carried out if the diagnosis is suspected.

41.   Hypertrophic pyloric stenosis   **Answers: B D**

Pyloric stenosis presents with projectile vomiting and has a male predilection. It typically presents in the sixth week of life and there is sometimes a family history. If there has been persistent vomiting, the child may be dehydrated and have hypokalaemia and a metabolic alkalosis. A test feed with clinical examination is still the technique to identify pyloric stenosis. However, ultrasound may identify the hypertrophy in up to 90% of cases.

42.   Abdominal pain   Answers: A B C D

Abdominal pain in a four-year-old infant can be due to a myriad of causes, many of them outside of the abdomen. Intestinal atresia is not a cause of abdominal pain in a four year old as it would present in the first few days of life.

43.   Hirschsprung's disease   Answers: A B C E

Hirschsprung's disease is a congenital abnormality characterised by the absence of ganglion cells in the myenteric plexus of the autonomic nervous system. The disease almost always involves the rectum and spreads for a variable distance proximally. It can in rare instances involve the entire intestine. Presentation in the adult is well described. It also has an association with Down's syndrome. Hirschsprung's disease is treated by resection of the aganglionic segment and colo-anal reconstruction (a 'pull-through' procedure).

44.   A term infant   Answers: A D E

Average sized term infants require 150 ml/kg of formula feed per day. This will provide about 100 calories/kg per day (the basic nutritional requirement). When a newborn infant undergoes surgery and requires intravenous fluids, the requirements are 100 ml of water/kg/day as well as 3 mmol of sodium and 2 mmol of potassium/kg/day. An infant undergoing surgery is under stress, and is at risk of hypoglycaemia. Therefore, a solution of 10% dextrose with 0.9% saline, to which is added 10 ml of potassium per 500 ml, will meet the infant's basic maintenance needs.

95% of term infants should pass meconium within the first twenty-four hours. Failure to do so might indicate a diagnosis of Hirschsprung's disease.

45.   Carcinoma of the prostate   Answers: B C

Carcinoma of the prostate is the commonest adult male tumour in the USA where opportunistic screening is common. It is second to lung cancer in the UK. It is more common in African-Americans and in general in the black population. The risk is 9-fold if two first-degree relatives are affected.

46.   Renal cell carcinoma   Answers: B D

Renal cell carcinoma (RCC) is associated with von Hippel-Lindau disease where patients are generally younger and may have bilateral tumours. The commonest symptom is haematuria (60%). The classic triad of haematuria, loin pain and a palpable mass only occurs in 10–15% of patients with RCC.

47.   Prostate cancer   **Answers: A C E**

Clinically this man has a T3 prostate cancer. Even though he has lower urinary tract symptoms it is important to biopsy the prostate as hormonal therapy may improve matters. Further, TURP may miss prostate cancers, as 70% arise in the peripheral zone which is not resected. A bone scan is indicated even if the PSA is normal, as a poorly differentiated tumour may be non-PSA producing. Treatment can be delayed until biopsy results are available except in emergencies, such as spinal cord compression. Diethylstilboestrol is generally regarded as second-line treatment due to its thrombo-embolic complications.

48.   Radiolucent stones   **Answers: C E**

All calcium-containing stones are radiopaque. Urate, xanthine and matrix calculi are radiolucent. Cysteine calculi have a ground-glass appearance.

49.   TURP   **Answer: A**

Although recurrent prostatitis may be treated with TURP, the results are disappointing and it is not an absolute indication. There is little correlation between residual volumes and renal impairment.

50.   Prostatitis   **Answers: B C**

Acute bacterial prostatitis may require a TURP if a prostatic abscess has formed. Chronic bacterial prostatitis requires a four week course of antibiotics. In younger patients with chronic abacterial prostatitis, doxycycline may be used although many patients do not respond. Prostatodynia has no diagnostic investigations.

51.   Concerning renal transplantation   **Answers: C E**

Transplanted kidneys are usually sited in an extraperitoneal position. A right donor kidney is more technically demanding to graft due to the short, right renal vein. A living donor transplant has a higher survival benefit than a cadaveric transplant, equivalent to a 10% benefit at five years.

52.   Colonoscopic surveillance   Answer: B

Current evidence suggests that patients with extensive disease (splenic flexure or more proximal) for > 8 years duration are most at risk and should be surveyed by 1–2 yearly colonoscopy. Patients with more distal disease, even if long-standing, have a much lower risk of developing cancer and can be screened less frequently i.e. every five years. Age of onset of colitis *per se* and the presence or absence of extraintestinal manifestations of disease, are not indications for regular colonoscopic surveillance. Patients with confirmed severe dysplasia are best managed by proctocolectomy with or without restoration of intestinal continuity because of the risk of occult or overt carcinoma in up to a third of cases.

SECTION 2 – EMQS

Investigation of carotid artery disease

61. A   Duplex Doppler ultrasound of carotid arteries
62. C   CT scan of head
63. E   Transcranial Doppler ultrasound

Duplex Doppler ultrasound of the carotid arteries is the initial investigation of choice for carotid stenosis. It is the quickest and safest investigation for amaurosis fugax. Carotid angiography or MRA may be used subsequently to confirm the Duplex findings.

The 28-year-old with the dense stroke is most likely to have an intracranial bleed. Thus, a CT of the head would be the first investigation of choice.

Transcranial Doppler measures the flow in the middle cerebral artery and is thus useful in the intra-operative monitoring and investigation of post-endarterectomy neurological episodes. Duplex Doppler would also demonstrate patency of the carotid artery following endarterectomy.

Near infra-red spectroscopy measures intracerebral blood flow but is not currently used for intra-operative monitoring.

Leg ulcers

64. D   Post-phlebitic
65. C   Diabetic
66. A   Arterial

Leg ulcers often have multiple aetiologies. The aetiology is usually apparent from taking a clear history and identifying the site of the ulcer. The most common causes of leg ulcers are venous, arterial, diabetic, vasculitic (including rheumatoid arthritis) and neoplastic. Venous and post-phlebitic ulcers tend to be situated in the gaiter area and have sloping edges. Arterial ulcers have punched out edges and often occur at the extremities, e.g. toes. Diabetic ulcers often occur at the site of trauma or ill fitting shoes. Neoplastic ulcers have raised, rolled or everted edges and may occur anywhere.

Types of ulceration

67. Squamous cell carcinoma in a chronic venous ulcer	C	Marjolin's ulcer
68. Head injury	B	Cushing's ulcer
69. Major burns	A	Curling's ulcer
70. Major thoraco-abdominal trauma	D	Stress ulcers
71. Inflammatory bowel disease	E	Pyoderma gangrenosum

Marjolin's ulcers are squamous cell carcinomas that develop in long-standing chronic venous ulcers. Gastroduodenal stress ulcers follow major trauma or sepsis. The pathophysiology is unclear but is thought to relate to relative mucosal ischaemia, lack of oral alimentation, and altered gastric mucous barrier function. Specific forms of gastroduodenal stress ulceration include Cushing's ulcer which follows severe head injury, and Curling's ulcer which follows major burns. Pyoderma gangrenosum occurs in inflammatory bowel disease, more commonly in ulcerative colitis than Crohn's disease.

Surgical investigations

72. Hepatic hydatid cyst	B	Abdominal CT scan
73. Uncomplicated diverticular disease of the colon	F	Barium enema (double contrast)
74. Sclerosing cholangitis	D	ERCP
75. Choledocholithiasis	D	ERCP
76. Psoas abscess	B	Abdominal CT scan
77. Small bowel tumour	C	Small bowel follow-through
78. Colovesical fistula	F	Barium enema (double contrast)
79. Pancreatic necrosis	B	Abdominal CT scan

Hepatic hydatid disease characteristically results in complex cysts with septation and daughter cysts, and is best seen on CT. Double contrast barium enema is the most precise method of demonstrating the presence and extent of uncomplicated diverticular disease. ERCP defines ductal anatomical detail well, and may reveal the 'chain of lakes' of sclerosing cholangitis. Ultrasound may fail to show ductal dilatation or common duct stones. ERCP would provide a more definitive diagnosis and allow therapeutic manoeuvres for choledocholithiasis. No technique is certain to reveal a colovesical fistula, but cystoscopy and barium enema are the two most likely investigations to help. X-ray of spun urine following barium enema may also reveal barium radio-opacity. Pancreatic necrosis is not well visualised on ultrasound. Dynamic CT scans will show non-perfused pancreatic tissue.

Anatomy of the viscera and organs in the abdomen

80.	Is crossed by the inferior mesenteric vein	H	Kidney
81.	Has a mesentery attached to the pelvic brim	B	Ileum
82.	Has a venous drainage into the inferior vena cava	A	Supra-renal gland
83.	Has an umbilical attachment	G	Meckel's diverticulum
84.	Lies in the lienorenal ligament	F	Pancreas
85.	Has veins forming portosystemic anastomoses	D	Stomach

- The left kidney has the inferior mesenteric vein passing over its anterior medial border.
- The root of the mesentery of the small bowel is attached below to the brim of the pelvis over the left sacro-iliac joint.
- The right suprarenal gland drains into the inferior vena cava.
- Meckel's diverticulum is frequently either attached to the umbilicus directly or indirectly by a fibrous band.
- The tail of the pancreas lies in the lienorenal ligament touching the hilum of the spleen.
- The left gastric vein forms porto-systemic anastomoses through its ascending oesophageal branches with the hemi-azygos system.

Low back pain

86. F   Spondylolisthesis
87. B   Muscle strain
88. D   Osteoporotic collapse
89. G   Discitis
90. E   Metastatic disease

Spondylolisthesis commonly presents in teenage years with pain and hamstring tightness. This is not the same as a limited straight leg raise where the 'strain' is on the sciatic nerve.

Muscle strains are the most common cause of low back pain in fit young adults particularly if there has been some 'unaccustomed' exercise! A slipped disc is more likely to have been associated with radiation of the pain and symptoms of nerve root irritation.

Sprightly 88-year-olds often have osteoporosis and a simple stumble can cause an osteoporotic fracture with collapse. As she is getting better a more sinister explanation is unlikely.

In children who refuse to walk, a septic arthritis or osteomyelitis of the lower limbs must first be excluded, only then a diagnosis of discitis may be considered.

Although this man is relatively young his history of progressive increasing pain with radiation to the buttocks and cauda equina symptoms must make you concerned about a metastatic lesion.

Transitional cell carcinoma

91. A   TURBT
92. G   Nephroureterectomy
93. D   M-VAC chemotherapy

The diagnosis and treatment (in most cases) of a bladder tumour is a trans-urethral resection (TURBT). The standard treatment of a transitional cell carcinoma in either the kidney or ureter is a nephroureterectomy, as these tumours are often multifocal and surveillance of a ureteric stump is difficult. A cystectomy is contraindicated if enlarged pelvic lymph nodes are detected pre-operatively.

Neonatal surgical diagnoses

94. A   Hirschsprung's disease
95. G   Exomphalos
96. H   Midgut volvulus
97. B   Oesophageal atresia
98. C   Tracheo-oesophageal fistula

Hirschsprung's disease usually presents in the neonatal period with a history of delayed passage of meconium, abdominal distension and bile stained vomiting. The infant may well be shocked with impending enterocolitis. Hirschsprung's disease is more common in children with Down's syndrome (Trisomy 21).

Both gastroschisis and exomphalos are frequently diagnosed antenatally. The difference being in exomphalos, the liver is frequently outside the abdomen and the herniated organs are covered by an identifiable membrane.

Bile stained vomiting in a previously well infant should raise the suspicion of a mid-gut volvulus. A baby with oesophageal atresia is frequently born to a mother with a polyhydramnios. At birth the infant is unable to swallow even saliva which froths through the mouth and nose. Oesophageal atresia can occur with or without a tracheo-oesophageal fistula which itself can occur in isolation. When an infant feeds there may be aspiration of milk through the fistula into the lungs. Occasionally the infant may be several months old before the diagnosis is made.

END OF SYSTEM PAPER 1

1. Acute otitis media Answer: A

Acute otitis media is very common especially in children in whom presentation may be in the form of generalised malaise, pyrexia or GI upset. Otalgia and hearing loss are more common features in adults. The causative organisms are usually *Streptococcus pneumoniae* or *Strep. haemophilus.* The first-line treatment is a broad spectrum antibiotic e.g. amoxycillin. Myringotomy is only advocated once perforation has occurred. If the acute phase does not settle, a more chronic infection develops and in rare instances a cholesteatoma may form.

2. Oral cavity cancer Answer: E

The two main aetiological factors are excessive smoking and alcohol consumption. Men are more commonly affected and the median age of presentation is 60 years. The most common signs and symptoms are an ulcer, swelling, pain and a neck lump. The tumours usually arise in the salivary gutters of the mouth. Indications for surgery are failed radiotherapy, bony invasion and cervical metastasis. Chemotherapy has little role in the management of oral cavity malignancy.

3. Insulin Answers: A B

Insulin affects many organs and intra-cellular pathways. Insulin is synthesised by the β islet cells of the pancreas and is an anabolic hormone. It stimulates glucose storage but inhibits glucose production. In addition, it enhances protein synthesis and inhibits proteolysis. The uptake of glucose by the brain is independent of insulin.

4. Fat embolism Answer: E

Fat embolism is most common in patients with multiple closed fractures. It may also occur following burns and cardiac surgery. The clinical features of fat embolism include dyspnoea, mental confusion, restlessness and petechiae in the conjunctival folds and on the chest. There is no specific test for fat embolism but a fairly constant finding is hypoxaemia.

5. Charcot's triad Answers: C D E

Charcot's triad is strongly suggestive of ascending cholangitis and comprises fever, jaundice and abdominal pain. It has an associated mortality of 30%.

6.   Perforated duodenal ulcer   Answers: B D E
A perforated duodenal ulcer is usually found on the anterior surface of the first part of the duodenum. Patients often present with a localised or more generalised peritonitis but silent perforations do occur especially in elderly women. These may be treated conservatively. The operation of choice is patching greater omentum loosely tied over the perforation. In cases of massive perforation, a partial gastrectomy may be required.

7.   Primary peritonitis   Answers: A B D
Primary or spontaneous bacterial peritonitis is usually caused by haematogenous spread of a single bacterium, most commonly a Gram-negative bacillus such as *E. coli*. There is an increased incidence of primary peritonitis in cirrhosis, ascites and nephrosis. The ascitic fluid has an increased white cell count. Signs may be obscured in the presence of pre-existing ascites.

8.   Pancreatic carcinoma   Answers: B C
70–80% of pancreatic carcinomas arise in the head, neck, or uncinate process. CT usually gives more information than ultrasound. Features suggestive of irresectability include hepatic or lymph node metastases, ascites, invasion of the superior mesenteric vessels, portal vein and IVC. Typical radiological features on ERCP include localised stricturing of the main pancreatic and bile ducts, known as the 'double-duct' sign.

9.   Post-gastrectomy patient   Answers: B C D E
Gastrectomy is associated with post-gastrectomy symptoms in 20% of cases. These include biliary reflux, diarrhoea, early (hypovolaemic) and late (hypoglycaemic) dumping syndromes, anaemia and malnutrition (including calcium deficiency). A microcytic and macrocytic anaemia may also be seen. This is due to reduced iron and vitamin B_{12} absorption, respectively. Afferent loop syndrome is the result of kinking or creation of too long a loop (jejunal) following a polya gastrectomy.

10.   Crohn's disease   Answers: A B D
There are numerous extra-intestinal manifestations of Crohn's disease but the specific hepatobiliary complications of Crohn's disease include cirrhosis, cholangiocarcinoma and chronic active hepatitis. Amyloid deposits are found in a number of chronic disease states.

11. Crohn's disease
Answers: B C

The classical radiological features of Crohn's disease on small bowel imaging include mucosal ulceration and fissuring, thickening of the valvulae conniventes, fistulae to other intraperitoneal viscera or skin, luminal narrowing (with or without prestenotic dilatation) bowel wall oedema, and skip lesions. Intra-mural cysts are a feature of pneumatosis coli. Patients with Crohn's disease may have a shortened small bowel length due to previous resections.

12. Ulcerative colitis
Answers: A B D

Typical endoscopic features of ulcerative colitis include fine or coarse mucosal granularity, pseudopolyps, loss of the normal vascular pattern, mucosal oedema, contact bleeding, and mucosal ulceration. Microadenomas are associated with familial adenomatous polyposis coli. Deep fissuring ulceration with a cobblestone appearance occurs in Crohn's disease.

13. Familial adenomatous polyposis
Answers: B C

Gastric adenomas occur in 2–10% of patients with FAP, and duodenal adenomas in 30%. Hyperplastic gastric polyps are also common. Atrophic gastritis is not a recognised feature of the condition. Congenital hypertrophy of the retinal pigment epithelium is a common retinal abnormality occurring in FAP, but it is not pathognomonic of the condition. Uveitis is not a recognised feature of FAP. There is a 50–100 times increased risk of developing papillary thyroid cancer compared to the general population.

14. Carcinoid tumours
Answers: B D E

Carcinoid tumours occur in the vermiform appendix (40%), small intestine (mainly ileum) (20%), large bowel (mainly rectum) (20%), lung and bronchus (10%), and other sites (10%). Most carcinoids of the appendix and rectum are benign, and are incidental findings.

15. Rupture of oesophagus
Answers: A B

Traumatic rupture of the oesophagus has a high morbidity and mortality. Extravasation of swallowed air results in mediastinal emphysema, and unchecked mediastinal soiling results in mediastinitis. A Gastrografin swallow is the diagnostic modality of choice. Boerhaave's syndrome refers to spontaneous lower oesophageal rupture during vomiting. When perforation is due to oesophagoscopy the tear is usually near the level of the cricoid cartilage, resulting from crushing against the cervical spine, which is often osteoarthritic.

16. Phaeochromocytomas
Answers: D E F

90% of phaeochromocytomas are benign. 10% in adults and 25% in children are extra-adrenal in site: in the organ of Zuckerkandl, the para-aortic and paravertebral regions, and in the urinary bladder. Phaeochromocytomas are bilateral in 5–10% in adults and 25% in children.

17. Leg ulceration
Answers: A B C E

Classically, ulcers in the gaiter area of the leg are due to venous disease, however, arterial and diabetic ulcers may present there. Other causes include vasculitis (including rheumatoid arthritis and scleroderma), rheumatoid arthritis and allergic reactions. Ergot poisoning causes Raynaud's syndrome but not leg ulcers. Rare causes of leg ulceration include tuberculosis, syphilis, pyoderma gangrenosum, necrobiosis lipoidica and blood dyscrasias.

18. In vascular thrombosis
Answers: C D E

'Corraline clot' is a fine granular coral-like mass of platelets deposited on the endothelium and is otherwise known as 'white thrombus'. 'Propagative clot' is red, slippery, non-adherent, and particularly likely to break up and form emboli. It is otherwise known as 'red thrombus'. Aspirin, not anticoagulants, have an effect on platelet aggregation.

19. Cholecystectomy
Answer: A

At elective cholecystectomy, unsuspected biliary calculi are present in the common bile duct in 5–10% of patients, and retained calculi are found in 5–10% of patients after CBD exploration. Calot's triangle is bordered by the cystic artery, the common hepatic duct and the liver. Stones in the CBD have mostly arisen in the gall bladder. Primary bile duct calculi are uncommon. The overall success rate of ERCP in extracting CBD calculi is approximately 90%.

20. Acute dislocations of the shoulder
Answers: D E

Anterior dislocations account for almost all traumatic dislocations but posterior dislocations (2% of the total) may follow an electric shock or an epileptic fit. Fractures of the humeral neck or the greater tuberosity are fairly common. Damage to the axillary nerve is usually a neuropraxia and is noticed over a small area of the lateral aspect of the upper arm.

21.   Glasgow Coma Scale   **Answers: C E**

A history of drug abuse may affect the interpretation but not the assessment of the GCS. GCS uses the best motor response – in a patient with a spinal injury and a risk of neurological injury the best motor response is likely to be found in the upper limbs. Elective intubation involves the use of paralysing or sedative drugs which prevents one evaluating the GCS.

22.   Anal fissures   **Answers: C D**

The gold standard treatment of anal fissure is lateral sphincterectomy (division of the internal anal sphincter). GTN is effective in the treatment of anal fissure, but it heals only 40–60% of chronic anal fissures, however, recurrence rates are considerable.

23.   Surgical anatomy of the thyroid gland   **Answers: A B**

The thyroid gland has a definite fine capsule which allows a capsular dissection to preserve the recurrent laryngeal nerves. The superior parathyroid glands are more constant in position than the inferior parathyroid glands. Because of their embryological migration the inferior glands may be situated among the pre-tracheal lymph nodes or in the thymus as far as 10 cm from the thyroid. The middle thyroid veins are the least constant of the thyroid veins. The superior veins drain into the internal jugular vein, the inferior veins are very constant and drain into the brachiocephalic veins, and the middle veins are very variable and often multiple. Unilateral recurrent laryngeal nerve section results in the ipsilateral vocal cord lying motionless in the mid or cadaveric position. The voice is hoarse and weak. If both recurrent laryngeal nerves are divided, the glottic space is narrowed, and stridor develops. An emergency tracheostomy is necessary.

24.   Internal jugular veins   **Answers: All true**

The compartments of the jugular foramen are: anterior, containing the inferior petrosal sinus and IX; middle, containing X and XI; and posterior, containing the internal jugular vein as a continuation of the sigmoid venous sinus. The inferior petrosal sinus drains the cavernous sinus and is the first tributary of the internal jugular vein, which descends in the neck as the anterior component of the carotid sheath, and drains into the brachiocephalic vein on each side behind the sternoclavicular joint. The ansa loops anteriorly around the carotid sheath under the cover of the sternocleidomastoid muscle.

25.   The tongue   Answers: B C E

The sensory innervation to the tongue is from Vc and IX. The tongue deviates to the side of a hypoglossal nerve lesion on protrusion, is active during the first stage of swallowing, retracted by the styloglossus muscle, and contains the lingual tonsil in the dorsum of its posterior third.

26.   The scalp   Answer: E

The blood supply to the scalp is from branches of both the internal and external carotid arteries. There is no C1 dermatome. The aponeurosis of the scalp is separated from the epicranium by loose connective tissue (the plane of cleavage in scalping) facilitating gliding movements. It contains no lymph nodes. The occipitofrontalis muscle is supplied by VII.

27.   The ante-cubital fossa   Answers: B C

The ante-cubital fossa contains the posterior interosseous branch of the radial nerve (which leaves the fossa between the two heads of the supinator muscle) and the brachial artery (which lies lateral to the median nerve against the tendon of the biceps muscle). The artery bifurcates within the fossa into radial and ulnar arteries. Part of the roof is formed by the bicipital aponeurosis which separates the superficial median cubital vein from the contents of the fossa. The brachioradialis muscle and the medial edge of the supinator muscle form the floor.

28.   Extension of the fingers   Answers: All true

All muscles that insert into the extensor expansion extend the fingers at the interphalangeal joints; the lumbrical and interosseous muscles also flex the first metacarpophalangeal joints. The radial nerve is a branch of the posterior cord of the brachial plexus and innervates the long extensor muscles. The ulnar nerve supplies the two ulnar lumbrical muscles, and all the interosseous muscles. The two radial lumbrical muscles are supplied by the lateral digital branches of the median nerve.

29.   The serratus anterior muscle   Answer: B

The thoracodorsal nerve is vulnerable in axillary surgery because of its unprotected prominence on the posterior wall. The whole of the serratus anterior muscle (8 costal digitations: 1 & 2 into the superior angle; 3 & 4 whole vertebral border; lower 4 inferior angle) is used to protract the scapula whilst the bulky insertion into the lower angle of the scapula aids the trapezius muscle in rotation. The long thoracic nerve (of Bell), which is protected underneath the fascia covering the serratus anterior muscle, innervates the muscle, originating from the C5–7 roots.

30.   Upper end of the jejunum   Answers: A B D E

The jejunum has a thicker wall, less mesenteric fat, more mucosal circular folds, a wider lumen and fewer Peyer's patches than the ileum. These features allow the surgeon to distinguish between them at operation.

31.   The right suprarenal gland   Answers: A B C

The right suprarenal gland lies against the bare area of the liver, behind the inferior vena cava, separated from the 12th rib by the diaphragm. It receives blood from three sources including the inferior phrenic artery. The venous drainage is into the inferior vena cava by a very short vessel.

32.   The pancreas   Answers: B D

The head of the pancreas is related to the hilum but does not overlie the right kidney. The trans-pyloric plane transects the pancreas obliquely, passing through the mid point of the neck, with most of the head below the plane, and most of the body and tail above. The transverse mesocolon is attached to the head, neck and body of the pancreas. The uncinate process lies posterior to the superior mesenteric vessels, and the inferior mesenteric vein passes behind the body of the pancreas, where it joins the splenic vein.

33.   The epiploic foramen   Answers: A B C D

This is an important surgical area particularly for open cholecystectomy and gastrectomy where familiarity with all structures around the epiploic foramen is paramount, particularly those in the free edge of the lesser omentum. The lower boundary of the foramen is formed by the first part of the duodenum. The caudate lobe is the only part of the liver present in the lesser sac.

34.   The male urethra   Answers: A B

Rupture of the spongy (penile) part of the urethra leaks urine into the superficial perineal fascia (of Colles), which is continuous with the membranous fascia (of Scarpa) in the anterior abdominal wall. The penile urethra takes a 90° angle through the bulbar part. The corpus spongiosum invests the penile urethra.

35.   The L3 vertebra   Answers: All false

Flexion and extension take place between lumbar vertebrae. The left crus of the diaphragm is attached to the first two lumbar vertebrae and the iliolumbar ligament to the lateral process of the L5 vertebra. The central canal, at the level of the L3 vertebra, contains the cauda equina. The iliolumbar branch of the posterior division of the internal iliac artery supplies the L5 vertebra. Only paired segmental lumbar branches of the abdominal aorta supply L1–4 vertebrae.

36.   The hip joint   Answers: A B D
The rectus femoris muscle assists the iliopsoas muscle in flexion of the hip. The hamstring component of the adductor magnus muscle inserted into the adductor tubercle of the femur extends the hip. The iliopsoas muscle assists tensor fascia lata, and the gluteus medius and minimus muscles in medial rotation but, when the neck of the femur is fractured, the axis of rotation shifts laterally from the head to the shaft and iliopsoas becomes a lateral rotator. Flexion is limited by the soft tissues of the anterior abdominal wall.

37.   The knee joint   Answers: A B D E
The popliteus tendon penetrates the capsule and is covered by synovial membrane. The supra-patella bursa, although developing as an isolated cavity, later fuses with the joint space. The iliotibial tract is attached to a smooth round facet on the anterolateral aspect of the head of the tibia. The middle geniculate artery pierces the joint capsule to supply it and the cruciate ligaments. Flexion occurs in the upper compartment, rotation in the lower compartment of the knee.

38.   Dorsum of the foot   Answers: C D E
The dorsalis pedis artery lies between the extensor hallucis longus tendon medially, and the deep peroneal nerve laterally. The L5 dermatome lies over the medial half of the dorsum of the foot. The great saphenous vein is found anterior to the medial malleolus, and the lower limb of the extensor retinaculum passes under the medial longitudinal arch and blends with the plantar aponeurosis.

39.   Internal iliac artery   Answers: B C D E
The sigmoid colon is supplied by the sigmoid branches of the inferior mesenteric artery. Sacral radicular branches are given off by the lateral sacral arteries and feed into the anterior and posterior spinal vessels of the sacral segments of the spinal cord. Both the trochanteric and cruciate anastomoses are fed by descending branches of the superior and inferior gluteal arteries, whilst the iliolumbar and superior gluteal arteries contribute to the anterior superior iliac spine anastomosis.

40.   Groin hernias   Answer: E
Indirect inguinal hernias enter through the internal inguinal ring lateral to the inferior epigastric vessels. Direct inguinal hernias usually emerge through the medial aspect of the posterior wall of the inguinal canal. Sliding hernias may have caecum, sigmoid, or bladder forming part of the wall of the sac. Femoral hernias are more common in females, but inguinal hernias are overall more common than femoral hernias in women.

41.   Infant born at 32 weeks' gestation   Answers: C D

Premature infants do not always require ventilation in the first twenty-four hours after birth. Premature infants have a much higher insensible fluid loss than an adult, because of the thinner skin, and greater body surface area to weight ratio. This means that careful attention must be paid to the environment in which these infants are cared for. When infants require long-term venous access, it is occasionally necessary to operatively insert a central line into the internal jugular vein. Premature infants are at a high risk of developing necrotizing enterocolitis. Pyloric stenosis is known to occur in premature infants.

42.   Exomphalos   Answers: A B C E

Exomphalos has a frequent association with other structural and chromosomal abnormalities leading to a mortality rate in the region of 25% after birth. Herniated organs in exomphalos are covered by a membrane derived from the umbilical cord and therefore the bowel and liver are not damaged by being outside the fetal abdomen. The liver is frequently herniated in exomphalos. In small exomphalos defects, a loop of bowel may herniate into the umbilical cord, thus the umbilical cord clamp may involve this loop of intestine if placed too close to the infant's abdominal wall.

43.   Hydrocele of infancy   Answers: A B E

A hydrocele in an infant is due to a persistent patent processus vaginalis, which allows fluid to communicate between the abdomen and scrotum. The processus vaginalis may continue to obliterate in the first twelve months of a child's life, and the child can be observed until after this age. Repair is necessary if the hydrocele persists, or presents *de novo*. Hydroceles may also occur in females. Surgery involves simple division of the patent processus vaginalis. When the patent processus vaginalis does not extend as far as the testicle, the hydrocele fluid may not surround the testicle.

44.   Acute appendicitis   Answers: All true

Acute appendicitis is uncommon at the extremes of age. The diagnosis can be difficult and is often delayed in children under the age of five as they have difficulty in localising the site of pain as well as describing their symptoms. In this age group, the disease is often more aggressive. Many of these infants require intensive care peri-operatively. In a mentally handicapped child, the first evidence of appendicitis may be unexplained weight loss. Laparoscopy is a very effective means of operating on children of all ages.

45.   Prostatic carcinoma   Answers: A C E
Prostatic cancer has a rising incidence with age. Androgen suppression or androgen antagonists give symptomatic relief in disseminated carcinoma in about 75% of patients. Surgical castration reduces circulating androgen levels by about 95%.

46.   Bladder cancer   Answers: B E
Although the aromatic amines and other carcinogenic agents are a recognised cause of bladder cancer, health and safety measures have made this a rarity. The commonest world-wide cause of bladder cancer is *Schistosoma haematobium*. p53 mutations are associated with high-grade muscle-invasive bladder cancers and carcinoma in situ. The prognosis of carcinoma in situ is guarded, with approximately 50% developing muscle-invasive bladder cancer. Most bladder cancers (85%) are superficial and are treated endoscopically. Orthotopic bladder reconstruction causes metabolic abnormalities and therefore must not be used in patients with impaired renal function.

47.   Undescended testis   Answers: B C
The incidence of UDT in term infants is 3–4%. In preterm babies the incidence is 30%. 75% of UDT descend by one year and most of these descend in the first three months. Placement in the scrotum does not change the risk of tumour development but places the testis in a palpable position. Microscopic data have shown that spermatogenesis becomes impaired if orchidopexy is performed after one year. Laparoscopy is the investigation (and treatment) of choice for intra-abdominal testes.

48.   Benign prostatic hypertrophy   Answers: A B D
Tamsulosin and alfuzosin are α-blockers which relax the smooth muscle of the prostate and bladder neck. Tolterodine is an anti-cholinergic used in the treatment of detrusor instability. It may precipitate urinary retention. Finasteride is a 5 α-reductase inhibitor which reduces prostate size. Goserelin is used in the treatment of prostate cancer.

49.   Tumours   Answers: A B C
Circumcision in infancy is associated with an extremely low risk of developing penile cancer in adult life. There is no proven association between prostatic cancer and vasectomy.

50.   Rigid ureteroscopy   Answers: A B
Annual surveillance is not generally required for superficial bladder tumours as the incidence of an upper tract tumour is < 2%. Rigid ureteroscopy cannot adequately visualise the pelvi-calyceal system where tumours are more common than in the ureter.

ANSWERS – System Paper 2

51. Torsion of testis
Answers: B D

Colour Doppler is not 100% reliable, so if there is any suspicion then exploration must be carried out. Peak incidence is 14–18 years. Younger children are more likely to have a torted hydatid of Morgagni. Torsion of the testis is a surgical emergency. Most testis are viable up to four hours after the onset of torsion. There are reports of viable testis up to 72 hours, though this is more likely with intermittent torsion. Extra-vaginal torsion (torsion of the cord) occurs in utero or shortly after birth.

52. Hirschsprung's disease
Answers: C E

The abnormality in Hirschsprung's disease is aganglionosis to the large bowel. The abnormality starts at the anus and extends proximally. The male:female ratio is 5:1. The lumen of the aganglionic segment is narrowed, but the bowel proximal to this is grossly dilated. The aetiology of the enterocolitis that sometimes occurs in infants is obscure, but *Clostridium difficile* and *E. coli* endotoxin have been suggested.

Rectal bleeding

61. A Crohn's disease
62. G Meckel's diverticulum
63. B Solitary juvenile polyp
64. C Familial Adenomatous Polyposis
65. H Mid-gut volvulus

Rectal bleeding is a common symptom throughout childhood. Crohn's disease may present in many ways but is frequently associated with weight loss or linear growth failure in children. Meckel's diverticulum may present with acute GI haemorrhage leading to the typical 'brick red' coloured stool. The ulceration caused by the ectopic gastric mucosa within the Meckel's diverticulum may lead to lower abdominal pain.

Solitary juvenile polyps are relatively common, causing painless rectal bleeding. Occasionally the polyps may be multiple.

Familial adenomatous polyposis should be suspected in children presenting with rectal bleeding when there is a family history of early colorectal carcinoma in immediate family members. The polyps generally develop after puberty.

Mid-gut volvulus is frequently preceded by a history of intermittent colicky abdominal pain with or without bile stained vomiting. This diagnosis should always be considered in a child with bile stained vomiting and rectal bleeding.

Surgical investigations

66.	A suspected acutely obstructing large bowel cancer	A	Gastrografin enema
67.	Empyema of the gall bladder	E	Abdominal and pelvic ultrasound
68.	Colonic diverticular abscess	B	Abdominal and pelvic CT scan
69.	Terminal ileal Crohn's disease	C	Small bowel follow-through
70.	Colonic anastomotic leak on day 4 post-operatively	A	Gastrografin enema

An acutely obstructing large bowel cancer is best assessed with a Gastrografin (water soluble) enema. Colonoscopy is associated with an increased risk of perforation, and a barium enema perforation may result in a severe peritonitis. A barium enema clearly defines the presence and extent of colonic diverticular disease. A CT would identify an abscess associated with diverticular disease. Fat streaking and localised inflammatory changes would be seen. Acute and chronic gall bladder pathology is best seen on ultrasound. Small bowel pathology is presently not well seen on other forms of investigation other than follow-through contrast examinations. Early colonic anastomotic leaks are best assessed using gastrografin enemas; free intraperitoneal leakage of barium causes peritonitis.

Inflammatory bowel disease

71.	Irreversible peripheral neuropathy	E	Metronidazole
72.	Reversible infertility due to oligospermia	A	Sulphasalazine
73.	Osteoporosis	B	Corticosteroids
74.	Cataracts	B	Corticosteroids
75.	Hepatic fibrosis	C	Methotrexate
76.	Pneumonitis	C	Methotrexate

Metronidazole is associated with irreversible peripheral neuropathy and does not appear to be related to the dose or length of time of ingestion. The hepatic fibrosis and pneumonitis from methotrexate use is related to the total dose given. Osteoporosis and cataracts are well-known complications of corticosteroids.

Parathyroid glands

77.	Most lie adjacent to the cricothyroid notch close to the recurrent laryngeal nerve	B	Superior parathyroid glands
78.	When ectopic, may lie in the posterior mediastinum	B	Superior parathyroid glands
79.	Are derived from the third branchial pouch	A	Inferior parathyroid glands
80.	May lie anywhere from the mandible to the anterior mediastinum	A	Inferior parathyroid glands
81.	Are derived from the fourth branchial pouch	B	Superior parathyroid glands
82.	20% lie on or within the supra-sternal portion of the thymus	A	Inferior parathyroid glands

The inferior parathyroid glands, along with the thymus, are derived from the third branchial pouch. The superior parathyroid glands are derived from the fourth branchial pouch. The inferior glands are usually adjacent to the lower pole of the thyroid gland but may lie anywhere from the mandible to the anterior mediastinum. 20% lie on or within the supra-sternal portion of the thymus. The superior glands are normally found adjacent to the inferior thyroid artery just after it has started to branch, adjacent to the cricothyroid notch, and close to the recurrent laryngeal nerve. Overall, super-numerary glands occur in approximately 5% of the population.

Anatomy of joints in the head and neck

83.	Movements at the joint lengthen the vocal cords	D	Cricothyroid
84.	Is a secondary cartilaginous joint	C	Intervertebral disc
85.	Subserves a rotatory movement whose axis is outside the joint	B	Temporo-mandibular
86.	At which flexion of the head occurs	A	Atlanto-occipital
87.	Has a fibrocartilagenous intra-articular disc	E	Sterno-clavicular
88.	Stabilised by a transverse ligament	G	Atlanto-axial
89.	Is a saddle joint	F	Crico-arytenoid

- Rotatory movements at the cricothyroid joints tilt the thyroid cartilage forward elongating/tensing the vocal cords.
- Intervertebral discs are secondary fibrocartilagenous joints allowing movement.
- The axis of rotation of the mandible is not through the TMJ but through the lingula of the mandible, since the movement is compound, comprising contemporaneous protraction onto the glenoid eminence with flexion.
- Flexion of the head occurs at the atlanto-occipital joint.
- The sterno-clavicular joint has a fibrocartilagenous disc (the TMJ disc is fibroelastic).
- The atlanto-axial joint is stabilised by a transverse ligament which holds the odontoid process in register with a facet on the anterior arch of the atlas.
- The crico-arytenoid joints are typical saddle joints allowing rotatory and gliding movements over the shoulders of the posterior arch of the cricoid cartilage.

Anterior abdominal wall

90.	Division of the aorta into the common iliac vessels	B	L4 vertebral body
91.	Ureter	F	Sacro-iliac joint
92.	Femoral artery	D	Mid inguinal point
93.	Upper poles of the kidneys	J	12th rib
94.	External ring of the femoral canal	G	Below and lateral to the pubic tubercle
95.	L5 vertebral body	L	Trans-tubercular plane
96.	Termination of the spinal cord	A	Trans-pyloric plane
97.	Spleen	K	10th rib

- The aorta divides on the L4 vertebral body to the left and in front of the inferior vena cava
- The ureter crosses the pelvic brim at the sacro-iliac joint
- The femoral artery passes under the inguinal ligament at the mid-inguinal point
- The upper pole of the kidney lies on the 12th rib, on each side
- The external ring of the femoral canal lies below and lateral to the pubic tubercle
- The L5 vertebral body lies in the trans-tubercular plane
- The spinal cord terminates in the trans-pyloric plane at the lower border of the L1 vertebra
- The spleen lies on the left 9th, 10th and 11th ribs, posteriorly

Nerve damage

98. D Neurapraxia of the common peroneal nerve
99. C Median nerve neurapraxia
100.H Radial nerve neurotmesis
101.A Horner's syndrome
102.F Sciatic nerve injury

The peroneal nerve is very susceptible to pressure, and thus may result in a neurapraxia. Following a supracondylar fracture of a child's humerus, a neurapraxia of the median nerve is perhaps the most common neurological lesion but damage to the ulnar nerve is also common. If a surgical procedure is complicated by a nerve injury – a nerve transection (neurotmesis) must be considered, especially if the nerve was not visualised. A flail upper limb suggests a brachial plexus lesion which might well be associated with a Horner's syndrome if the sympathetic chain was involved. During a hip replacement, two forms of nerve injury are well documented: direct damage to the sciatic nerve at the level of the hip joint (more common) or pressure on the peroneal nerve at the neck of the fibula. During a posterior approach to the hip, the sciatic nerve is in particular danger.

Imaging

103.H CT scan
104.F DMSA scan
105.G DTPA scan

A non-contrast spiral CT with thin (5 mm) cuts will detect 'all' calculi. This imaging modality may be used when an IVU or ultrasound are contraindicated or impractical. Staghorn calculi require DMSA imaging to ascertain the split function of the kidneys. PUJ obstruction has a trimodal distribution: antenatal, teenagers (when they start drinking alcohol) and the elderly. A diuresis, in a patient with PUJ obstruction, worsens pain and should arouse suspicion of this condition.

END OF SYSTEM PAPER 2

1.   Anaplastic thyroid carcinoma   Answers: B C E

Histology of anaplastic thyroid carcinoma shows few or no differentiated structures, and has an extremely poor prognosis. Death occurs within one year of diagnosis in 90% of patients. It may be confused with lymphoma and biopsy (fine needle, core or open biopsy) is required. Anaplastic carcinoma of the thyroid usually presents with a hard, fixed mass and commonly invades the trachea, oesophagus, recurrent laryngeal nerves and carotid arteries.

2.   Submandibular gland excision   Answers: A C E

The structures to be avoided at the time of submandibular gland excision include the mandibular branch of the facial nerve, the hypoglossal and lingual nerves and the facial artery and retromandibular vein. Linguinal nerve damage results in ipsilateral anaesthesia and hemiplegia of the tongue. Hypoglossal nerve injury restricts the mobility of the tongue. Frey's syndrome (gustatory sweating) is a complication of parotid surgery.

3.   Normal function of the colon   Answers: A B C

The ascending and transverse colon are involved in the regulation of intra-luminal fluid volume as well as sodium and water absorption. The left colon is the site for final modulation of intra-luminal contents before evacuation. More than 90% of short chain fatty acids are taken up by colonic mucosal cells. Chloride absorption occurs by a passive energy independent mechanism, being absorbed together with sodium. Bicarbonate is secreted by the colon, by an energy requiring process. Bile salts are absorbed in the terminal ileum.

4.   Raised serum amylase levels   Answers: A D E

It is recognised that serum amylase levels may be raised in pancreatitis, perforated peptic ulcer, acute cholecystitis, intestinal strangulation, renal failure, ectopic pregnancy, dissecting AAA, and macroamylasaemias.

5.   Colonic diverticular disease   Answer: D

Diverticula occur between the mesenteric and the antimesenteric taeniae. The diverticula are of the pulsion type and consist of pouches of mucosa that have herniated through the circular muscle. The circular muscle of affected bowel is thickened, resulting in shortening. Asians have an increased incidence of right-sided colonic diverticular disease, and the disease tends to occur in younger patients than those with left-sided disease.

6.   Long-term effects of gastrectomy   Answers: A C D

Most patients who undergo a gastrectomy fail to regain their pre-op weight. Low serum calcium, vitamin C and iron levels are seen, as the hypochlorhydria interferes with their absorption. Due to diminished levels of intrinsic factor from the stomach, vitamin B_{12} deficiency develops. This may be corrected by three monthly injections of hydroxycobalamin.

7.   Full thickness rectal prolapse   Answers: B C D E

In adults, full thickness rectal prolapse is seen predominantly in females. Faecal incontinence may be a presenting feature but most commonly a prolapsing mass is described. Surgical treatment is complex, as numerous operations have been variably described. The prolapse may be repaired via perineal (e.g. Delorme's, rectosigmoidectomy) or abdominal approaches. The latter may be open or laparoscopic. They involve mobilising the rectum and suturing it to the sacral promontory or partially wrapping the rectum in a mesh.

8.   Carcinoid tumours   Answers: A C D E

Carcinoid tumours are neuroendocrine in origin. They commonly occur in the small bowel and 85% of appendix neoplasms are known to be carcinoid in origin. They can also occur in extra-intestinal sites such as the bronchus. A small proportion of patients with carcinoid tumours develop the carcinoid syndrome (flushing, bronchospasm and diarrhoea due to the secretion of 5-HT, bradykinin and histamine).

9.   Hepatic metastases   Answers: A B C

Several series show 25–30% 5-year survival rates following resection of colorectal hepatic metastases from colorectal cancer in the absence of other metastatic or recurrent disease. The best surgical results are achieved by resection along hepatic segmental lines. Although chemotherapy often slows or regresses tumour growth, it is not curative. Liver metastases are present in about 25% of patients at the time of diagnosis of the primary tumour. These lesions are relatively radio-resistant.

10.   Colorectal cancer   Answers: C D E

Colorectal cancer is thought to be inherited in only 10% of cases. Both metachronous and synchronous cancers occur in 2–5% of cases. Colorectal cancer is inevitable in cases of untreated FAP, with an average age of presentation in the third decade. The cumulative lifetime risk approaches 100%. Of all prognostic factors for colorectal cancer, the clinical stage of disease is the most important.

11.   Barium enema   Answers: B F

Barium enema is not as sensitive for the assessment of polyps as colonoscopy, especially if they are small. Barium enema is more sensitive for the assessment of diverticular disease than colonoscopy, and is superior at showing the extent and pattern of disease. Imaging and macroscopic appearances of the bowel are normal in collagenous colitis. It is a histological diagnosis and requires colonic biopsies. Double contrast studies (barium and air) give greater mucosal detail and are superior to single contrast studies. Barium enema, though often demonstrating the appendiceal lumen, is not used for the assessment of appendiceal pathology.

12.   Acalculous cholecystitis   Answers: A D

Acute acalculous cholecystitis can arise spontaneously, but is especially common in ITU patients following major trauma, surgery or sepsis. It is thought to be related to bile stasis. Factors contributing to increased bile viscosity include fever and dehydration. Diagnosis is made on suspicion of those patients at risk and the findings of gall bladder wall thickening and pericholecystic fluid on ultrasound in the absence of gallstones.

13.   Inflammatory bowel disease   Answers: B C E

In Western populations, the approximate prevalence of Crohn's disease is 1 in 1500, and that of ulcerative colitis is 1 in 1000. The prevalence of IBD is the same in different social classes. There is an increased incidence of both ulcerative colitis and Crohn's disease in Jews living outside Israel, suggesting an aetiological mix of environmental and genetic factors.

14.   Crohn's disease   Answers: A B E

The approximate incidences of involvement are: ileocaecal only 40%, colon only 25%, ileum only 25%, extensive small bowel disease 5%, and miscellaneous (e.g. confined to the anorectum; oral; gastric) 2%.

15.   Splenic preservation   Answers: A B C E

Omental patch repair is helpful by allowing additional support for sutures which otherwise often tear out and worsen bleeding. Topical thrombogenic agents used include gelatin, gelatin sponge, fibrin glue, and collagen. Induced hypotension is never used and may seriously risk life in an already haemorrhaging patient. Partial splenectomy is useful where damage is localised. Other techniques used include direct suture repair using atraumatic needles if tears are superficial, and mattress sutures with Teflon buttresses.

16.   Lumps in the groin   Answers: D E

Femoral hernia necks are located below and lateral to pubic tubercle. Enlarged inguinal lymph nodes may be associated with a cough impulse in the presence of a coincident hernial sac but never give rise to a cough impulse in their own right. Varicoceles are usually non-tender. Clinical examination enables the examiner to 'get above' a cyst of canal of Nuck. Hydroceles of the cord are clinically irreducible.

17.   Child's classification   Answers: A E

Child's classification of hepato-cellular function in cirrhosis includes details of serum bilirubin, serum albumin, the presence of ascites, encephalopathy, and nutrition. Patients are scored into groups A, B or C, with increasing mortality risk from surgery.

Child's classification of the severity of chronic liver disease			
Group designation	A	B	C
Bilirubin	< 35	35–50	>50
Albumin	> 35	30–35	<30
Ascites	None	Mild–moderate	Severe
Encephalopathy	None	Mild	
Advanced			
Nutrition*	Good	Moderate	Poor
Risk of surgery	Good	Fair	Poor

*   Pugh's modification replaces nutrition with prothrombin time

18.   Cholesterol gallstones   Answers: A E

Cholesterol stones are about 75% cholesterol by weight, usually contain a pigmented centre, and constitute about 75% of human gallstones. Most are radiolucent. Pigment stones, which are more common in sickle cell disease, are usually hard and spiculated, and composed of calcium bilirubinate and pigment polymers. Approximately 50% are visible on AXR. Overall, only about 10% of all gallstones are radio-opaque.

19.   Leg lymphoedema   Answers: A C D

Lymphoedema is an accumulation of tissue fluid as a result of a fault in the lymphatic system. It principally affects the legs (80%). However, it may be found in the arm, face and genitalia. Lymphoedema may be divided into primary and secondary. Secondary lymphoedema in Western countries is usually the result of surgical excision or radiotherapy to lymph nodes. On a world-wide scale, infection is much more common. The worm *Wuchereria bancrofti* causes filiariasis leading to lymphoedema.

20. Right carotid endarterectomy   Answers: B C

Current indications for carotid endarterectomy include ipsilateral amaurosis fugax or contralateral TIAs or a recent stroke (< 6 months) with 70% or greater internal carotid artery stenosis. Carotid endarterectomy is not currently indicated for stenosis less than 70%. Asymptomatic carotid surgery is currently the subject of randomised clinical trials and, as yet, surgery for asymptomatic carotid is not definitely indicated.

21. Right common carotid artery   Answer: E

The right common carotid artery is a branch of the brachiocephalic artery and bifurcates at the level of the upper border of the lamina of the thyroid cartilage undercover of the sternocleidomastoid muscle. It lies posterior to the thyroid gland and anterior to both the cervical sympathetic chain and the phrenic nerve on the scalenus anterior muscle, the latter is separated from the artery by prevertebral fascia.

22. Turning head to the left   Answers: C D

The head is turned using the contralateral sternocleidomastoid muscle, stimulated by impulses passing in the spinal accessory nerve. The movement takes place at the atlanto-axial joint about a vertical axis through the odontoid process of the axis, and is limited by the vertical alignment of the two attachments of the contralateral sterno-cleidomastoid muscle (contralateral mastoid process and sterno-clavicular joint).

23. The palatine tonsillar bed   Answers: D E

The palatine tonsil lies in the oropharynx, in a pit floored by the superior constrictor muscle through which the IX passes. The tonsil is supplied by the tonsillar branch of the facial artery. Venous blood drains firstly into the tonsillar venous plexus, then into the pharyngeal venous plexus and thence into the external palatine vein (a bleeding point after tonsillectomy).

24. The Eustachian tube   Answers: B C

The pharyngotympanic tube drains the middle ear into the nasopharynx by piercing the pharyngobasilar fascia. The cartilaginous part gives attachment to the tensor veli palatini muscle. It opens on swallowing under the action of the salpingopharyngeus and tensor palati muscles and is obstructed by an enlarging pharyngeal tonsil (adenoids).

25. The true vocal folds   Answer: E

The true vocal folds have a stratified squamous epithelium, innervated by the recurrent laryngeal branch of X, and are formed by the vocal ligament (the free edge of the quadrangular membrane forms the false vocal cord). The cords are adducted by the lateral cricoarytenoid muscle and lengthened and tensed by tilting the thyroid cartilage downwards and forwards by contracting the cricothyroid muscle.

26. The basilic vein   Answers: A C D E

The basilic vein is a continuation of the ulnar stem of the dorsal venous arch in the hand. It lies medial to the biceps tendon in the cubital fossa and is medial to the medial cutaneous nerve of the forearm in the arm. It pierces the deep fascia in the middle of the arm, and becomes the axillary vein at the lower border of the teres major muscle.

27. Full abduction of the arms   Answers: A B C D

Abduction of the arms is initiated by the supraspinatus muscle over the first 15°. The deltoid muscle then takes over and, at about 90°, the arm is laterally rotated mainly by the infraspinatus muscle (both the supra-spinatus and infraspinatus muscles stabilise the shoulder joint by tightening the rotator cuff). The scapula is then rotated by the combined actions of the trapezius and the inferior fibres of the serratus anterior muscles. The teres major muscle is a medial rotator and not part of the rotator cuff.

28. The scaphoid bone   Answers: A B C D

The scaphoid articulates with the radius and since it transmits weight from the hand to the radial head it is commonly fractured during falls. When the fracture line severs the blood supply to the proximal fragment, avascular necrosis of the latter is a common complication. Tenderness in the anatomical snuffbox is initially the only clinical sign of the fracture before radiological evidence of osteonecrosis develops (two weeks later). The flexor retinaculum takes origin from the tubercle of the scaphoid and ridge on the trapezium. The adductor pollicis muscle has an origin from the capitate, not the scaphoid; thus adduction of the thumb is unimpaired and pain free after scaphoid fracture.

29. The knee joint   Answers: A C (D)

The knee is locked in full extension by forward (medial) rotation of the lateral femoral condyle on the tibia. The axis of rotation is through the medial femoral condyle, which is fixed by the taut anterior cruciate ligament. All collateral, cruciate and posterior ligaments ultimately become taut on full extension. The iliotibial tract is also taut when the knee is extended but this stabilises the joint rather than limiting extension.   *ACL attached to lat fem. condyle*

30. In the lumbosacral plexus   Answers: A B D

Sympathetic grey rami connect with all spinal nerve roots. The nervi erigentes originate from S2, 3 and often 4. The lumbosacral trunk (L4/5) passes anterior to the alar of the sacrum, undercover of the common iliac vessels, and joins the S1 ventral ramus above the piriformis muscle. The adductor muscles are supplied by L2–4 roots of the lumbar plexus. They develop by medial migration from the flexor (hamstring) compartment, and are therefore supplied by anterior divisions.

31. The patella reflex   Answers: A B

The patella reflex is mediated by the femoral nerve formed from the posterior divisions of the L2–4 anterior spinal rami, and is thus lost after femoral nerve and L2–4 dorsal root damage. T12 cord lesions result in an upper motor neurone lesion with exaggerated reflexes. Dorsal column lesions only affect central sensory processing since collaterals subserving spinal reflexes are preserved.

32. The ilioinguinal nerve   Answers: A D E

The ilioinguinal nerve lies posterior to the kidney and enters the inguinal canal by piercing the transversus abdominis and internal oblique muscles (not by passing through the internal ring). It is motor to these two muscles, and thus to the conjoint tendon. The nerve passes with the iliohypogastric nerve in the anterior abdominal wall between the transversus and internal oblique muscles close to McBurney's point and, if damaged after gridiron incision, will paralyse the muscle fibres in the conjoint tendon, which may give rise to an indirect inguinal hernia.

33.   The linea semilunaris of the rectus sheath   Answers: A E

The semilunar line marks the lateral margin of the rectus sheath passing from the pubic tubercle to the costal cartilage at the tip of the 9th rib, which overlies the fundus of the gall bladder on the right. The inferior epigastric vessels and medial umbilical ligament cross the line posteriorly below the arcuate line before ascending in the posterior compartment of the rectus sheath. The anterior abdominal wall would be greatly weakened by cutting along the semilunar line both physically and functionally as the nerve supply to the rectus abdominis muscle and overlying skin would be interrupted. The line is formed by the interdigitation of the aponeuroses of the external and internal oblique muscles above the arcuate line; below the line the aponeuroses of these two muscle and that of transversus abdominis are layered on one another and pass anterior to the rectus abdominis muscle to form the anterior layer of the sheath.

34.   The processus vaginalis   Answer: D

The processus vaginalis is a parietal peritoneal sac which passes through the internal ring of the inguinal canal in the foetus, but which is normally obliterated after birth except for a small part which becomes the tunica vaginalis of the testis. The testis descends through the canal as a retroperitoneal structure and is therefore outside and behind the processus vaginalis. In cases of a persistent processus vaginalis, indirect inguinal hernias ensue.

35.   In the bony pelvis   Answers: B D

In the natal cleft, the sacral cornua are important surface markings for the sacral hiatus through which a needle is passed for epidural anaesthesia. Direct inguinal hernia protrude above and medial to the pubic tubercle. The femoral canal has the lacunar ligament as its medial wall. The sacral spine guides a needle to the pudendal canal for per vaginum perineal anaesthesia by pudendal nerve block. The trans-tubercular plane is an important landmark for lumbar puncture and transects the L5 vertebra (the supra-cristal plane, which passes through the L4 lumbar spine, can also be used).

36.   Radiological features of osteoarthritis   Answers: B C D

The four classic signs are loss of joint space, bony sclerosis and cyst formation in the weight-bearing areas of the joint, and osteophyte formation at the joint margins. Periarticular erosions are classically found in rheumatoid arthritis.

37.   **Mesentery of the small bowel**   **Answers: B D**
The veins in the mesentery are all tributaries of the portal system; the
nerves are post-ganglionic sympathetic fibres and pre-ganglionic
parasympathetic axons. The superior mesenteric artery supplies the mid-
gut including the large bowel as far as the left colic flexure; the branch
to the lower part of the ascending colon, caecum and appendix running
in the mesentery is the ileocaecal artery. The root of the small bowel
mesentery extends from a point to the right of the L2 vertebra, at the
duodeno-jejunal junction, to the left sacroiliac joint. The transverse
mesocolon lies anterior to the small bowel mesentery.

38.   **The diseased enlarging ovary**   **Answers: A C E**
The diseased ovary irritates the adjacent peritoneum supplied by the
obturator nerve. Pain is thus referred to the skin innervated by the
cutaneous branches of the anterior division over the adductor
compartment of the thigh (medial aspect). As the ovary enlarges into the
abdomen, it may be palpable in the recto-uterine pouch.

39.   **Prolapsed L5/S1 intervertebral disc**   **Answers: A C D**
Nerve root involvement is suggested by pain radiating below the knee.
It is worse when the nerve is stretched as with the sciatic stretch test or
when intra-abdominal pressure is raised as with straining at stool,
coughing or sneezing. Urinary retention is a worrying sign but is not
infrequently secondary to pain, analgesic medication and bedrest.
Before this can be assumed a full neurological examination must be
performed and if there are concerns regarding a cauda equina syndrome,
further investigations must be carried out. An absent ankle jerk implies
some nerve root damage but on its own it does not demand surgical
intervention.

40.   **Avascular necrosis in the absence of injury**   **Answers: A D E**
Avascular necrosis of bone is a recognised complication of sickle cell
disease, decompression sickness and Gaucher's disease (a familial
disorder common in Ashkenazi Jews). It is also seen after irradiation and
may also be due to drugs (particularly corticosteroids, alcohol and
immunosuppressants). Although haemophilia A and B are associated
with arthritis, they are not recognised as causing avascular necrosis.
Hunter's disease is a glycogen storage disorder and is not associated with
avascular necrosis.

41.   **Osteochondritis**   **Answers: A B D**
Osteochondritis in the upper limb is commonly found in the scaphoid
(Preiser's disease), lunate (Kienbock's disease) and capitulum (Panner's
disease).

42.   In gastroschisis   Answers: B E

There is no evidence that delivering babies with gastroschisis by Caesarean section has any advantage to the baby or the mother. The bowel that has herniated from the fetal abdomen is not covered by membrane derived from the umbilical cord and is therefore in contact with the irritant amniotic fluid. After the bowel has been reduced into the abdomen after birth, the bowel frequently does not work for several weeks due to inflammation and oedema, therefore the infant requires TPN. If it is not possible to reduce the bowel immediately, a silastic pouch ('silo') may be sutured around the rim of the defect. This is suspended above the baby, who is paralysed and ventilated and kept supine for several days. The bowel can be gently squeezed back into the abdomen over this time, before the baby is returned to the operating theatre to have the silo removed and the abdominal wall repaired. Gastroschisis usually occurs as an isolated abnormality.

43.   Inguinal hernia in infancy   Answers: B D

Inguinal hernia occurring in infancy is usually of the indirect variety and is due to the presence of a widely patent processus vaginalis into which bowel or ovary may herniate. The processus vaginalis normally obliterates at about 40 weeks' gestation. Therefore, inguinal hernia is more common in infants born prematurely. In small infants presenting with inguinal hernia in the first few weeks of life, the risk of strangulation is approximately 1 in 3. Waiting until an infant is about 10 kg in weight (approximately one year of age) places a significant number of infants at risk of bowel, testicular or ovarian damage. Infants with inguinal hernia require a simple herniotomy (ligation of hernial sac) and not a herniorrhaphy.

44.   Bile stained vomiting   Answers: A C

Bile stained vomiting is a serious sign in any child and surgical causes need to be excluded. Bile stained vomiting occurs when the cause of the obstruction is distal to the ampulla of Vater. This is the case with both mid-gut volvulus (obstruction is in the third part of the duodenum) and intussusception. In pyloric stenosis and gastro-oesophageal reflux, the vomit is generally altered feed and the 'vomiting' of oesophageal atresia is that of unaltered milk.

45.   Positions for an ectopic testis   Answers: B D
A maldescended testis is one which has failed to reach the normal low position in the scrotum. Maldescent can be either arrested descent (cryptorchidism), where the testis is found at some point along the line of normal descent (intra-abdominal, inguinal canal, superficial inguinal pouch or high scrotum), or loss commonly in a position not on the normal line of descent, ectopic, penile, superficial inguinal, or femoral.

46.   Staging of prostate cancer   Answers: A D
The TNM classification is used to stage prostate cancer. T1 is not palpable or visible. Tumours are stage $T1_a$ if < 5% chips involved and $T1_b$ if > 5% chips involved following TURP. T2 is a tumour confined within the prostate. Extra capsular extension not involving the seminal vesicals is stage $T3_a$. Seminal vesical involvement is stage $T3_b$. T4 is when the tumour is fixed or invades adjacent structures.

47.   Muscle-invasive bladder cancer   Answers: A C D E
Organ confined prostate cancer is common in this population. A standard cystoprostatectomy will also treat incidental organ-confined prostate cancer. Prior to female orthotopic bladder reconstruction, the bladder neck must be biopsied. Lymph node involvement pre-op is a contraindication to surgery. If however lymph nodes are detected at operation a few surgeons advocate continuing with the operation and administering adjuvant (CMV or M-VAC) chemotherapy post-operatively.

48.   Macroscopic haematuria   Answers: B C D E
Haematuria from BPH is common but it is a diagnosis of exclusion. Patients must be fully investigated in all cases of macroscopic haematuria.

49.   Testicular tumour   Answers: A B C G
This male has a testicular tumour until proved otherwise. Often this condition presents with trauma, directing the patient's attention to the testicles. A scrotal ultrasound may demonstrate the lesion and exclude a tumour or microcalcification associated with intra-tubular germ cell neoplasia (ITGCN) on the opposite side. An abdominal CT is mandatory to exclude retroperitoneal nodal disease and a CXR to exclude any metastasis. The treatment is radical orchidectomy, via an inguinal approach to prevent scrotal contamination.

50. Acute urinary retention   **Answer: B**

Digital rectal examination prior to urethral catheterization has a tendency to grossly overestimate prostate size. Suprapubic catheterization should be a last resort, particularly in patients with frank haematuria where a bladder cancer could seed in the suprapubic tract. PSA may be elevated in cases of acute urinary retention and should not be measured at this stage. Renal ultrasound is not a first-line investigation and should only be considered if renal function tests are abnormal or in patients with haematuria (combined with a plain KUB). Urine cytology is not indicated in acute urinary retention.

51. Extracorporeal shock-wave lithotripsy   **Answers: A C D E**

ESWL is contraindicated in pregnancy and in patients with aortic aneurysms where the aneurysm directly lies in the 'blast path'. Caution must be taken with patients with pacemakers or those with clotting abnormalities. Steinstrasse (stone-street) is a recognised complication of ESWL. It can be avoided if a ureteric stent is inserted prior to treatment especially where stone bulk exceeds 1.5 cm.

52. Bladder calculi   **Answers: A B C**

Patients with bladder calculi usually present with irritative symptoms (frequency, urgency) rather than poor flow and hesitancy. A plain radiograph or ultrasound examination is required to make the diagnosis.

SECTION 2 – EMQs

Jaundice

61.	Bilirubin in the urine	C	Post-hepatic jaundice
62.	History of recent foreign travel	B	Hepatic jaundice
63.	Positive Courvoisier's sign	C	Post-hepatic jaundice
64.	Associated pancreatitis	C	Post-hepatic jaundice
65.	Pruritus	C	Post-hepatic jaundice
66.	Intake of hepatotoxic drugs	B	Hepatic jaundice
67.	History of fever, rigors and sweats	C	Post-hepatic jaundice

Associations with pre-hepatic jaundice include the presence of urinary urobilinogen, the absence of urinary bilirubin, and a family history of haemolytic syndromes. Associations with hepatic jaundice include a history of recent foreign travel, alcohol or drug abuse, recent blood transfusion, or ingestion of hepatotoxic drugs (halothane, chlorpromazine). Associations with post-hepatic jaundice include bilirubin in the urine, a positive Courvoisier's sign (extra-hepatic duct obstruction), pruritus, a history of fever, sweats and rigors (cholangitis), and a history of dark urine and pale stools.

Anatomy of abdominal vasculature

68.	Porto-systemic anastomosis	C	Left gastric vein
69.	Lies posterior to the first part of the duodenum	F	Gastroduodenal artery
70.	Drains into the splenic vein	A	Inferior mesenteric vein
71.	Lies posterior to the inferior vena cava	D	Right renal artery
72.	Drains the suprarenal gland	E	Left renal vein
73.	Supplies the caecum	J	Ileocolic artery
74.	Lies to the left of the superior mesenteric vein	B	Superior mesenteric vein
75.	Supplies the fundus of the stomach	K	Splenic artery

- The left gastric vein is continuous with the hemiazygos system through the oesophageal branches.
- The gastroduodenal artery is liable to erosion from duodenal ulcer as it lies behind the first part of the duodenum.
- The inferior mesenteric vein drains into the splenic vein.
- The right renal artery lies posterior to the inferior vena cava (whereas the common iliac veins lie posterior to the arteries).
- The left suprarenal gland drains into the left renal vein (along with the left gonadal vein).
- The ileocolic artery supplies the caecum and appendix.
- The superior mesenteric artery lies to the left of the vein, anterior to the uncinate process of the pancreas.
- The short gastric branches of the splenic artery passing in the gastrosplenic ligament supply the fundus of the stomach.

Anatomy of the inguinal canal

76.	Inguinal and lacunar ligaments	D	Floor
77.	Internal oblique and the aponeurosis of the external oblique	A	Anterior wall
78.	Conjoint tendon and fascia transversalis	C	Posterior wall
79.	Internal oblique and transversus abdominus muscles	B	Roof

Anatomy of the joints in the upper limb

80. Has an intra-articular ligament coursing through the joint   A   Shoulder

81. Is a saddle joint   G   Carpometacarpal

82. Is stabilised by an annular ligament   C   Superior radio-ulnar

83. Movements at this distal joint are the reciprocal to those at the proximal joint   H   Acromioclavicular

84. Is an articulation between three bones   B   Elbow

85 Has collateral ligaments which limit extension   F   Interphalangeal

86. Has an articular disc included in the proximal articulating surface   E   Wrist

- The shoulder joint has the tendon of the long head of the biceps muscle invested in synovial membrane running over the head of the humerus to attach to the supra-glenoid tubercle.
- The first carpometacarpal joint is a saddle joint allowing flexion, abduction, adduction, extension, rotation, and opposition.
- The annular ligament holds the head of the radius against the radial notch of the ulnar.
- Movements at the acromioclavicular joint are the reciprocal of those at the sternoclavicular joint.
- At the elbow joint, the ulna and radius articulate with the trochlea and capitulum of the humerus, respectively.
- At each interphalangeal joint, the two collateral ligaments lie obliquely across the joint, with the proximal attachment more dorsal than the distal. They thus become taut on extension halting further movement once the finger has straightened.
- The proximal articular surface at the wrist joint comprises the head of the radius and the articular disc which holds the lower ends of the radius and ulna together. This disc separates the wrist joint from the inferior radio-ulnar joint, in which it forms a distal articulating surface for the head of the ulna before attaching medially the ulnar styloid.

Bone disease

87. B   Avascular necrosis
88. F   Osteosarcoma
89. C   Rickets
90. A   Paget's disease
91. G   Osteochondroma

Steroids are a potent cause of avascular necrosis – which is painful in its own right although it is also a recognised cause of osteoarthritis. Bow-legs in a 2-year-old may be normal but in the presence of expanded metaphyses, a rickety rosary, failure to thrive and general lassitude and muscle weakness – rickets must be considered.

In an adult, increasing deformity with or without pain is often associated with Paget's disease – if it affects the skull, it may be associated with deafness. Spinal stenosis may also be seen. Osteosarcomas generally present in the second and third decades with swelling, pain, tenderness and loss of function. Osteochondromas occur around the same areas but usually produce much more discrete swellings – they should stop increasing in size at skeletal maturity.

Renal tract calculi

92. A   ESWL
93. C   Nephrectomy
94. B   Percutaneous nephrostomy

Stones ≤ 2 cm in diameter, that lie within the kidney, are usually treated with ESWL. Percutaneous nephrolithotomy (PCNL) is the treatment of choice for (i) Steinstrasse (fragments of stones following ESWL, they have the appearance of a 'stone street' in the ureter), (ii) stones ≥ 2 cm (or ≥ 1 cm in lower pole calyx) or (iii) those within the kidney. Stones in the lower pole calyx have poor clearance rates and thus PCNL is the preferred option. A staghorn calculus is treated with PCNL followed by ESWL (to residual fragments) or by open surgical removal if the kidney is functioning i.e. ≥ 15% split function on DMSA scanning or by nephrectomy if the split function is ≤ 15%. Obstructed infected kidneys need immediate drainage either by percutaneous nephrostomy (from above) or insertion of stent (from below).

Colorectal surgery

95. F   Abdomino-perineal resection
96. E   Sub-total colectomy
97. H   Hartmann's procedure

The first case is of a man with a recurrence of his anal carcinoma. He has undergone chemoradiotherapy which has failed. The only treatment for his continued bleeding is surgery in the form of an abdomino-perineal resection.

The second case is of a young lady with a flare up of her ulcerative colitis, failed medical treatment and development of a toxic megacolon. In this instance, the surgical option is a sub-total colectomy as she is at imminent risk of perforation. Her rectum is not excised, as this would add greater length to the surgery and increase her morbidity. In addition, as she is young the possibility of an ileo-anal pouch in the future should be left open to her.

The third case is of a man with a probable perforated sigmoid carcinoma and single metastasis to the liver. The carcinoma of mass should be resected and the nodule on the liver biopsied. A primary anastomosis in the presence of gross faecal contamination would be unwise. However, purulent peritonitis is itself not an absolute contraindication to a primary anastomosis. This should only be performed by experienced surgeons and the majority would cover with a loop ileostomy.

Abdominal disease

98.	Intra-abdominal desmoids	D	Familial adenomatous polyposis
99.	Ankylosing spondylitis	C	Ulcerative colitis
100.	Enteroenteric fistulae	A	Crohn's disease
101.	Perianal sepsis	A	Crohn's disease
102.	Pyoderma gangrenosum	C	Ulcerative colitis
103.	Colovesical fistula	B	Diverticular disease

Entero-enteric fistulae are more likely to complicate Crohn's disease than diverticular disease. Diverticular disease accounts for approximately half of all colovesical fistulae, and Crohn's disease comprises only about 15–20%. Pyoderma gangrenosum, ankylosing spondylitis, and toxic megacolon are more common in ulcerative colitis than in Crohn's disease. Anal pathology is much more prevalent in Crohn's disease.

END OF SYSTEM PAPER 3

1.   Otitis media   **Answers: All true**
Middle ear infection is one of the commonest sources of a brain abscess (temporal, cerebellum). This may subsequently give rise to clinical features of raised intracranial pressure, cranial neuropathies (III–VII) and visual disturbance. Sudden deafness may be caused by middle ear effusion.

2.   Posterior triangle of the neck   **Answers: B C**
The great auricular nerve turns round the lateral border of sternocleidomastoid muscle outside the triangle. The posterior belly of the omohyoid muscle and its intermediate tendon pass diagonally through the triangle (they are palpable, often being confused with both the upper trunk of the brachial plexus and the suprascapular nerve), and the clavicular (intermediate) and acromial (lateral) branches of the supraclavicular nerves course through the roof. Lying medially, outside the triangle, are the roots of the brachial plexus sandwiched between the scalenus posterior and medius muscles. The vertebral artery lies within the pyramidal space inferiorly before ascending through the foramen transversarium of the C6–C1 vertebrae.

3.   Chorda tympani nerve   **Answer: A**
The axons conveying taste over the anterior two-thirds of the tongue and secretomotor fibre to the submandibular and sublingual salivary glands (the parotid is innervated by IX) are found in the chorda tympani nerve. This nerve courses across the tympanic membrane beneath the mucous membrane of the middle ear after leaving the facial canal approximately 0.5 cm above the stylomastoid foramen. It exits the middle ear by passing through the petrotympanic fissure medially and runs forwards on the medial side of the spine of the sphenoid bone. The nerve, therefore, is not related to the parotid gland and escapes injury when VII nerve is compressed within the most distal part of the facial canal.

4.   Medullary thyroid cancer   **Answers: B C D**
Medullary thyroid cancer is sporadic in nearly 90% of cases. The other cases are familial and associated with MEN Type II. Medullary thyroid cancer is derived from parafollicular C cells and produces calcitonin which is used as a tumour marker. In addition, 5-HT, carcino-embryonic antigen, prostaglandin and prolactin are secreted by the tumour. Sporadic medullary thyroid cancer is usually solitary and unilateral, but hereditary forms are bilateral and multi-centric.

5.   Ludwig's angina   Answers: A B C

Ludwig's angina is a severe spreading cellulitis (infection of the submandibular, sublingual and submental spaces) caused by β–haemolytic streptococcus. It is usually caused by dental sepsis. It may cause dyspnoea, dysphagia and dysphonia. The priority is to secure the airway and treat with intravenous antibiotics. The infected spaces should be decompressed and the infected tooth removed.

6.   The nasopharynx   Answers: B D

The nasopharynx contains the pharyngeal tonsil (adenoid), salpingopharyngeal fold, and the pharyngeal recess adjacent to the internal carotid artery. The pyramidal fossae lie in the laryngopharynx. The pharyngeal branch of Vb, coming from the pterygopalatine ganglion, supplies the mucosa of the nasopharynx.

7.   Lateral swellings of the neck   Answers: A D

Lateral swellings of the neck include lymph nodes, salivary glands, branchial cysts, cervical ribs, carotid body tumours (chemodectomas), cystic hygromas, sternocleidomastoid tumours, arteriovenous fistulae, and lateral thyroid lobe lesions.

8.   Elevated parathyroid hormone   Answers: A C D

Parathyroid hormone raises serum calcium by increasing osteoclastic activity in the bones (causing bone resorption). It acts on the proximal and distal renal tubular cells so causing increased excretion of phosphate, calcium, sodium, potassium and bicarbonate. It decreases the excretion of magnesium and hydrogen ions. The net result is a fall in the serum phosphate level. Elevated parathyroid hormone causes osteitis fibrosa cystica (subperiosteal erosions on the radial aspect of the middle phalanges and a 'pepper pot' skull), polyuria, polydipsia, hypertension, peptic ulceration, acute pancreatitis and vague psychiatric symptoms.

9.   Mandibular nerve   Answers: D E

The anterior division of Vc has one sensory branch (the buccal nerve to the skin of the cheek and mucosa of the vestibule). All other branches are motor to the muscles of mastication. The lower jaw teeth are supplied by the inferior alveolar branch of the posterior division of Vc. The buccinator muscle is supplied by VII. Unopposed contraction of the contralateral lateral pterygoid muscle deviates the jaw to the side of the lesion during protrusion. None of the muscles of the pharynx are supplied by the anterior division of Vc, so dysphagia is not a feature of damage to this nerve.

10.   Meckel's diverticulum   **Answers: B C E**

Meckel's diverticulum is a remnant of the vitello-intestinal duct that connects the mid-gut to the yolk sac in embryological life. It lies on the antimesenteric border of the small bowel, and is supplied by a terminal branch of the superior mesenteric artery. It is a true diverticulum and the muscle coat is continuous with that of the ileum. Ectopic gastric epithelium may ulcerate, bleed or perforate. The commonest complication in adults is obstruction. The next most common complication is inflammation. In children, Meckel's diverticulum may cause obstruction and bleeding.

11.   Gallstone ileus   **Answer: D**

Gallstone ileus follows spontaneous perforation of the gall bladder into the gastrointestinal tract. Offending calculi usually impact in the distal ileum just proximal to the ileocaecal junction, which is the narrowest part of the small bowel. Obstruction is usually incomplete, making it difficult to diagnose preoperatively. Dilated small bowel loops and air in the biliary tree may be seen on AXR, but only occasionally is the obstructing calculus seen (10% cases).

12.   Arm lymphoedema   **Answers: A B D E**

The causes of arm lymphoedema are similar to those of leg lymphoedema. They include idiopathic causes, familial predisposition, surgery or radiotherapy to the axillary lymph nodes or metastatic infiltration.

13.   Duodenal ulcers   **Answers: A C E**

Duodenal ulcers are associated with *H. pylori* infection, excess acid secretion, smoking, NSAIDs and have an association with blood group O. Blood group A is associated with gastric cancer. Sucralfate may be used to treat them symptomatically.

14.   CT scan for head injury   **Answers: A D**

A CT scan is indicated if there is a fluctuating level of consciousness, presence of focal neurology, a deteriorating GCS or a score of less than 8.

15.   Crohn's disease   **Answers: A C D**

Typical endoscopic features of Crohn's disease include mucosal erythema, aphthous ulceration, loss of the normal vascular pattern, mucosal oedema, and deep fissuring ulceration with a cobblestone appearance. Microadenomas are associated with FAP. Pseudo-membranes are endoscopic features of pseudomembranous colitis.

16.   Rectal cancer   **Answers: C D E**

Distal intra-mural spread of rectal cancer is usually < 1 cm, so that a distal clearance of 2 cm is now considered adequate clearance for the majority of rectal cancers. The mesorectum contains an abundance of lymphatic and vascular channels. Malignant cell deposits have been found in lymphatic vessels up to 5 cm distal to the lower edge of rectal cancers. This has formed the basis of the argument for total mesorectal excision for rectal cancers. Irrigation of divided bowel ends with cytotoxic solutions such as chlorhexidine or iodine reduces local tumour recurrence in uncontrolled series. There are no randomised controlled trials to date.

17.   Hesselbach's triangle   **Answers: A B**

Hesselbach's triangle is the thin and weak part of the posterior wall of the inguinal canal covered only by transversalis fascia and peritoneum, through which direct inguinal hernias arise. The borders are the inferior epigastric artery, the inguinal ligament and the lateral border of the rectus abdominis muscle.

18.   Epigastric hernias   **Answers: A C D**

Epigastric hernias are multiple in about 30% of cases, and usually contain extraperitoneal fat, although they can sometimes contain small bowel. They are frequently irreducible, but are often more easily seen than felt. They are usually small and are repaired by excision of the extraperitoneal fat and sac, and a Mayo-type repair. Meshed repair is rarely required, but should be considered if the defect is large and the surrounding tissues are lax.

19.   Acute ulcerative colitis   **Answers: A B E**

Typical radiological features of acute ulcerative colitis on plain AXR include loss of haustral fold pattern, mucosal irregularity or ulceration, tubular shaped colon (lead pipe appearance), and absence of faecal residue within the actively inflamed part of the colon. Left-sided faecal loading is common in constipated patients. The 'beak sign' is seen on an instant enema in sigmoid volvulus.

20.   Inflammatory bowel disease   **Answers: B C D**

Endoscopic visual appearances alone sometimes allow one to differentiate between ulcerative colitis and Crohn's disease, however there is a large overlap in macroscopic findings. Definitive diagnosis requires histology, and even with histology the diagnosis is indeterminate in 10–15% of cases. An 'instant' enema is performed without bowel preparation. It is helpful if the anatomical extent of disease needs to be determined at initial presentation in order to guide appropriate management. Colonoscopy should only be performed when the disease is mildly active. Proximal colonic stool on plain AXR in a patient with ulcerative colitis suggests that the proximal large bowel is not significantly inflamed.

21.   Colorectal cancer   **Answer: D**

The incidence of invasive cancer in colorectal polyps is dependent on both polyp size and polyp type. Overall, the incidence in polyps < 1 cm is approximately 1%, in polyps 1–2 cm is approximately 10%, and in polyps > 2 cm is approximately 50%. Polyps in the rectum have a higher risk of malignancy than elsewhere in the colon. Villous adenomas have a greater risk of malignant change than tubular adenomas of the same size. According to the 'adenoma-carcinoma sequence', the majority of colorectal carcinomas arise in adenomatous polyps, but only a small proportion of polyps will become malignant.

22.   Inferior mesenteric vein   **Answers: A B E**

The inferior mesenteric vein drains the rectum through the superior rectal vein. The former lies superficially, immediately below the peritoneum and to the left of the inferior mesenteric artery. It therefore crosses in front of all structures in the left infracolic compartment. After crossing over the left renal vein, under the body of the pancreas, it joins the splenic vein (the portal vein is formed downstream, by the confluence of the splenic vein and superior mesenteric vein).

23.   The lesser omentum   **Answers: B C D E**

The right and left gastric arteries supply the lesser omentum as they lie between the two leaves of peritoneum. The free edge of the lesser omentum is attached to the first 2 cm of the first part of the duodenum below and the fissure of the ligamentum venosum above. The common hepatic duct is joined by the cystic duct to form the common bile duct in the free edge of the lesser omentum.

24.   Anorectal lesions   Answers: A C D

Anorectal lesions associated with HIV-infected patients include: Kaposi's sarcoma, rectal ulceration, lymphoma, neurofibromata, anal fissure, anal fistula, peri-rectal abscess, squamous cell carcinoma and condylomata acuminata. Apocrine hidrocystoma is a rare apocrine tumour unrelated to HIV.

25.   The ischiorectal fossae   Answers: All true

Infection from one fossa may spread across the midline through the retrosphincteric space of the anococcygeal raphe posteriorly, but the anterior recesses extending above the perineal membrane remain separate. The base of each fossa is formed by skin and superficial fascia and may be easily incised to drain ischiorectal abscesses. The inferior rectal nerves and internal pudendal vessels are not usually damaged since they arch high in the roof.

26.   Carcinoid syndrome   Answers: A B C E

The most prominent cutaneous manifestation of carcinoid syndrome is paroxysmal flushing (occurs in 75% of patients). It generally affects the face and central trunk. Flushing may be precipitated or exacerbated by hot food, chocolate, alcohol, cheese and stress. Systemic symptoms preceding or accompanying paroxysmal flushing include: abdominal pain, diarrhoea, bronchospasm, hypotension and wheezing. Although the tumours are frequently unresectable, debulking has been shown to provide palliative relief. Symptoms may also be improved by octreotide (somatostatin analogue).

27.   Dermatomyositis   Answers: A B E

Dermatomyositis has a 25% association with malignancy. The earliest cutaneous finding is oedema and erythema of the eyelids, causing a colour change (pinkish purple) and is termed a heliotrope rash. The most common malignancies associated with dermatomyositis are carcinoma of the ovary, breast, lung, cervix and GI tract. Dermatomyositis has been reported to precede development of the neoplasm by five years. Treatment of the malignancy results in improvement of the cutaneous changes.

28.   Fat embolism   Answers: C E

Fat embolism is often a clinical diagnosis substantiated by the blood gases which show hypoxia and hypocapnia. Fat globules may be found free or within macrophages in the blood, sputum and urine. Restlessness, agitation with a tachycardia and tachypnoea are common clinical signs.

29.   Bony metastatic disease   Answers: A B D

Metastases arising from a lung primary have a poor prognosis (metastases from renal cell carcinoma in contrast have one of the best prognoses). Prophylactic internal fixation should certainly be considered for any symptomatic (and some asymptomatic) lesions in a weight bearing bone. Treatment will depend on the site and histological nature of the primary.

30.   Virchow's triad   Answers: B D

Virchow's triad reflects changes promoting venous thrombosis and includes endothelial damage, altered blood constituents, and alteration of venous blood flow (from stasis or turbulence).

31.   Abdominal aortic aneurysms   Answers: A D

Abdominal aortic aneurysms occur about four times more commonly in males. The incidence of aortic aneurysms is rising in Western countries. They can be safely observed if asymptomatic and < 5.5 cm in size. Above this size, the risk of rupture rises exponentially and patients are offered surgery if fit enough to tolerate the procedure. The operative mortality for ruptured aneurysms remains at least 50%, and for elective surgery < 5%. 98% of AAA are infra-renal.

32.   The radial artery   Answers: A B C

The radial artery passes distally, after leaving the cubital fossa, medial to the biceps tendon, and anterior to the insertion of the pronator teres muscle. At the wrist, the artery passes across the floor of the anatomical snuff box over the trapezium, and enters the hand between the two heads of the first dorsal interosseous and the oblique and transverse heads of the adductor pollicis muscles. In the palm, it anastomoses with the ulnar artery forming the deep palmar arch.

33.   The femoral artery   Answers: A B C E

The surface marking of the femoral artery is the mid-inguinal point which lies medial to the position of the deep inguinal ring, which is at the mid-point of the inguinal ligament. The perforating branches of the profunda femoris artery supply the hamstrings and branches of the circumflex femoral arteries (contributing to the trochanteric anastomosis) and feed the femoral head through subretinacular branches. The femoral artery is subcutaneous in the femoral triangle, separated from skin by the fascia lata, and passes through the hiatus of the adductor magnus muscle into the popliteal fossa.

34.   The abdominal aorta   Answers: A C E

The aorta enters the abdomen under the median arcuate ligament at the level of the T12 vertebra, and divides into the common iliac arteries on the L4 vertebra. The cisterna chyli lies undercover of the right crus of the diaphragm, with the azygos vein on the right and the aorta to the left. In its course through the abdomen, the aorta gives off the three single ventral gut arteries and passes under the left renal vein.

35.   The popliteal fossa   Answers: A B

The roof of the popliteal fossa is formed by the fascia lata. Within the apex of the fossa, the sciatic nerve divides into common peroneal and tibial branches (but may divide higher), the former lies either against, or under the medial edge of the biceps femoris muscle, and the deepest structure is the popliteal artery. The sural nerve pierces the deep fascia half way down the leg.

36.   The sciatic nerve   Answers: All false

The sciatic nerve appears in the gluteal region below the lower border of the piriformis muscle, deep to the lower medial quadrant, and lateral to the inferior gluteal vessels. In its descent, it is separated from the capsule of the hip joint anteriorly by the obturator internus tendon, and the gemelli muscles.

37.   Carotid endarterectomy   Answers: All true

The 7th, 9th, 10th and 12th cranial nerves can be damaged during carotid surgery. Post-operative haematomata may cause stridor. Surgical trauma to the carotid sinus nerve may cause post-operative hypertension. This hypertension is usually self-limiting, though some centres use local anaesthesia as a prophylactic measure.

38.   The biceps tendon   Answers: A C D

The musculocutaneous nerve (C5, 6) is a branch of the lateral cord of the brachial plexus and supplies biceps. Each C5 and C6 spinal nerve is formed from dorsal (sensory) and ventral (motor) roots, mediating the afferent and efferent reflex arcs, respectively. Each spinal nerve divides into a dorsal and ventral ramus. The C5/6 ventral rami form the upper trunk of the brachial plexus. The lateral cord is formed from anterior divisions of the upper (C5/6) and middle (C7) trunks. Thus, neither the medial cord nor the middle trunk mediates the reflex.

39.   The triceps tendon reflex   Answers: C E

The radial nerve (C7/8) is a branch of the posterior cord of the brachial plexus and supplies the triceps muscle. Each C7 and C8 spinal nerve is formed from dorsal (sensory) and ventral (motor) roots, mediating the afferent and efferent reflex arcs. Each spinal nerve divides into a dorsal and ventral ramus. The C7/8 ventral rami form the middle and lower trunks of the brachial plexus. The posterior cord is formed from posterior divisions of all trunks. Thus, neither the lateral cord (anterior divisions), T1 ventral root, nor the upper trunk (C5/6) mediate the reflex.

40.   Avascular necrosis   Answers: A D E

Avascular necrosis is a complication of interruption of the blood supply to a bone by a fracture or dislocation. Susceptible bones are the femoral and humeral heads, the femoral condyles, the capitum (when avulsed), the proximal pole of the scaphoid, the lunate and the talus. The blood supply to the femoral head arises from the joint capsule. The femoral head is susceptible after an intracapsular (subcapital) but not an extra capsular (inter-trochanteric) fracture.

41.   Oesophageal atresia   Answers: All true

Oesophageal atresia is a complex congenital abnormality which is frequently associated with other structural abnormalities including vertebral, cardiac, renal and limb abnormalities (e.g. the VATER association). Oesophageal atresia can occur without tracheo-oesophageal fistula. When there is a long gap between upper and lower pouches (greater than approximately four vertebral bodies) definitive reconstruction of the oesophagus may be delayed until the child is beyond one year of life. Maternal polyhydramnios is a feature of oesophageal atresia.

42.   Acute respiratory distress   Answers: A B C E

Acute appendicitis may cause acute respiratory distress in a small child if there is widespread peritonitis with secondary pleural effusions. Crush injury to the abdomen may cause acute respiratory distress due to diaphragmatic rupture or oesophageal rupture. Congenital diaphragmatic hernia may in rare instances present in a child of this age. Young children frequently place objects in their mouth and inhale them. This should clearly be excluded in a child with sudden respiratory collapse.

43.   Infantile hypertrophic pyloric stenosis   Answers: B E
The metabolic upset with pyloric stenosis is typically a hypokalaemic hypochloraemic metabolic alkalosis. Although the metabolic disturbance is quite typical, the diagnosis should be made on clinical grounds and blood samples monitored to assess resuscitation. A test feed is usually used to aid diagnosis. Alternatively, an ultrasound may be helpful. Males are more frequently affected than females. Jaundice is an association in about 10% of children with pyloric stenosis.
At operation a number of approaches are described to the pyloric olive including the supra-umbilical approach which leaves minimal scarring in the long-term.   *C - umbilicus should be excluded*
                                  to avoid staph. infec:

44.   Congenital lymphoedema   Answers: A B C D
Congenital lymphoedema is caused by abnormality of the superficial lymphatics and is more common in women. It often does not manifest until the patient is in his or her twenties or thirties. Lymphovenous anastomosis depends on dilated distal lymphatics, possibly after a radical groin dissection. The Charles' or Homans' operations which remove the oedematous subcutaneous tissue have a limited but specific role in the management of lymphoedema.

45.   The prostate gland   Answers: All false
The seminal vesicles drain into the vas to form the common ejaculatory ducts which empty into the prostatic urethra. The prostatic venous plexus lies outside the capsule and thus 'shelling' of the prostate from inside the capsule is a relatively avascular procedure. The prostate lies above the urogenital diaphragm and is separated from the rectum by the recto-vesical fascia (of Denonvilliers).

46.   Base of the bladder   Answers: All true
On the base of the bladder in the male, the vas lies uppermost and loops medially over the ureters, which separate the seminal vesicle from the vas. In the female, the cervix and anterior vaginal wall are attached to the base of the bladder.

47.   The right kidney   Answers: A D
The upper pole of the right kidney lies on the diaphragm and lateral arcuate ligament, separated from the 12th rib by the costo-diaphragmatic space. The lower pole lies on both the iliohypogastric and ilioinguinal nerves. The sympathetic trunk and medial arcuate ligament lie medial to the kidney.

48.   Acute pancreatitis   Answers: B D E
Gallstones account for about 40% of cases of acute pancreatitis in the UK, and alcohol about 25% of causes. Other causes include post-ERCP, following trauma, drugs (e.g. azathioprine, corticosteroids, thiazide diuretics), cardiopulmonary bypass, mumps and Coxsackie viruses, hypercalcaemia, hyperlipidaemia, polyarteritis nodosa, uraemia, and pancreatic divisum.

49.   Metastatic prostatic cancer   Answers: B C D E
Metastatic prostate cancer is treated with hormonal therapy. Diethylstilboestrol is effective and is generally used as second-line treatment due to the risks of thrombosis (aspirin must be taken concomitantly).
Bicalutamide (Casodex) is a form of hormonal therapy for prostate cancer. It has a structure similar to testosterone and works by blocking and preventing the binding of testosterone to receptors on the surface of prostate cancer cells.

50.   first-line investigations   Answers: A B D G
Plain KUB X-ray and IVU are both correct but only one is necessary. IVUs are generally quicker to obtain than ultrasound, but cannot differentiate a renal cyst from a tumour. If a filling defect is detected in the renal parenchyma, ultrasound or CT is then indicated. CT scanning is not a first-line investigation.

51.   Pelvi-ureteric junction obstruction   Answers: A D
Pelvi-ureteric junction obstruction is one of the more common disorders seen in infancy and childhood. It may occur as a result of intrinsic (morphological changes in smooth muscle and excess collagen), extrinsic or secondary causes (severe vesicoureteric reflux, urinary tract obstruction).
The male:female ratio is 5:2 and left:right is 5:2. PUJ obstruction is best detected with diuretic renography, i.e. DTPA or MAG-3 scanning with a diuretic (frusemide). No intervention is necessary in utero unless there is oligohydramnios. Post-natally a pyeloplasty should be carried out to preserve renal function if the abnormality persists.

52.   Stones which form in acidic urine   Answers: A C
Staghorn calculi, (also known as struvite) are composed of magnesium, ammonium and phosphate. They form when urine pH > 7. They are associated with Proteus and other Gram-negative organisms which contain the enzyme urease. This results in the splitting of urea into ammonium ions, thus alkalising the urine.

Hernias

61.	Triangle of Petit	D	Lumbar
62.	Greater sciatic notch	E	Gluteal
63.	Pelvic floor	G	Perineal hernia
64.	Linea semilunaris	B	Spigelian
65.	Linea alba	A	Epigastric
66.	Obturator canal	C	Obturator
67.	Lesser sciatic notch	E	Gluteal

Lumbar hernia occur through either the inferior lumbar triangle of Petit (bounded by the iliac crest, the posterior edge of the external oblique, and the anterior edge of the latissimus dorsi) or the superior lumbar space (bounded by the 12th rib, the lower border of the serratus posterior inferior, and the anterior border of the sacrospinalis and the internal oblique). The others are self-explanatory.

Polyps

68.	Are usually a consequence of a severe episode of ulcerative colitis	E	Inflammatory polyps
69.	Are hamartomas	C	Peutz–Jeghers polyps
70.	May cause hypokalaemia	B	Villous adenomatous polyps
71.	Have the greatest malignant potential of all colonic polyps	B	Villous adenomatous polyps
72.	Are the commonest type of polyp seen in Familial Adenomatous Polyposis	A	Tubular adenomatous polyps

Villous adenomas frequently present with blood and mucus per rectum. When large, mucus secretion is great and hypokalaemia may occur. Villous adenomas have the greatest malignant potential of all colorectal polyps. Peutz–Jeghers polyps have no malignant potential themselves, but are associated with an increased risk of other malignant gut polyps. Metaplastic polyps are thought to have an extremely low malignant potential. Inflammatory polyps have no malignant potential.

ANSWERS – System Paper 4

Anatomy of the urogenital system

73.	Lies superior to the ureter	E	Vas deferens
74.	Transmits the ovarian vessels	F	Suspensory ligament of the ovary
75.	Has an internal sphincter which contracts during ejaculation	C	Urethra
76.	Transmits the dorsal vein of the penis	H	Perineal membrane
77.	Is separated from the rectum by peritoneum	A	Uterus
78.	Attaches the ovary to the uterus	B	Ligament of ovary
79.	Intervenes between the uterus and pubic symphysis	D	Bladder

- The vas lies above the ureter, as the latter enters the bladder.
- The ovarian vessels are transmitted by the suspensory ligament of the ovary (infundibulopelvic fold).
- Contraction of the internal sphincter of the male urethra prevents retrograde ejaculation into the bladder. After destruction of the sphincter at prostatectomy, ejaculation into the bladder occurs.
- The perineal membrane supports the penis and is pierced by the urethra and dorsal vein of the penis.
- The uterus is separated from the rectum by the pouch of Douglas.
- The ligament of the ovary is attached to the lateral wall of the uterus just below the isthmus of the Fallopian tube. It is the fibrosed remnant of the gubernaculum.
- The bladder intervenes between the uterus and pubic symphysis.

Knee injuries

80. F   Tibial plateau fracture
81. C   Patellar fracture
82. A   Injury to the medial meniscus
83. B   Anterior cruiate rupture
84. E   Medial ligament rupture

A valgus stress to the knee applied by a car bumper is likely to result in bony damage (a tibial plateau fracture) whilst a similarly directed force during a game of football is more likely to lead to rupture of the medial ligament. With complete rupture of this ligament, gross instability is noted at the time of injury and on weight bearing. As the joint has been disrupted, there is no discrete effusion, although the area may be swollen and bruised. Swelling due to medial meniscal injury usually takes some hours to become apparent. However, an anterior cruciate ligament rupture with the classical 'pop', produces a haemarthrosis rapidly.

Site of arterial disease

85. A   Lower aorta
86. H   Right superficial femoral artery

The heavy smoker is most likely to have an aortic occlusion causing impaired flow to the internal iliac arteries (Leriche's syndrome). The diabetic patient is most likely to have a right superficial femoral artery occlusion.

Pelvic vascalature

87.	Accompanies the ureter	G	Internal iliac artery
88.	Drains the middle third of the ureters	C	Gonadal veins
89.	Is a branch of the posterior division of the internal iliac artery	A	Superior gluteal artery
90.	Runs in the transverse cervical ligament (cardinal)	H	Uterine artery
91.	Communicates with the vertebral venous plexus	F	Lateral sacral veins
92.	Forms the medial umbilical ligament	B	Superior vesical artery
93.	Supplies the prostate gland	E	Inferior vesical artery
94.	Drains into the hepatic portal system	D	Superior rectal vein

- The ureter enters the pelvis by crossing anterior to the bifurcation of the common iliac artery and accompanies the internal iliac artery as far as its bifurcation into anterior and posterior divisions.
- The middle third of the ureters are supplied by the gonadal arteries and drained by the gonadal veins.
- The superior gluteal artery is the largest branch of the posterior division of the internal iliac artery.
- The uterine artery runs in the base of the broad ligament. The condensation of connective tissue around the uterine vessels forms the transverse cervical ligament attaching the cervix to the lateral pelvic wall, thereby stabilising the uterus.
- The lateral sacral veins directly communicate with the vertebral venous plexus by valveless tributaries, capable of carrying metastases from pelvic tumours to the vertebrae.
- The fibrosed continuation of the superior vesical artery is the vestige of the foetal umbilical artery.
- The inferior vesical artery supplies the prostate gland.
- The superior rectal vein drains into the inferior mesenteric vein and thus into the portal system.

Benign prostatic hyperplasia

95. E Retropubic (open) prostatectomy
96. C TURP
97. C TURP

The morbidity in patients with very large prostates (> 100 g) is less if open retropubic prostatectomy is performed rather than a TURP, as this reduces operation time and avoids excessive fluid absorption during prolonged surgery. Finasteride is a useful treatment in men with large (> 40 g) prostates. It also reduces prostatic bleeding. Catheterization is not indicated in simple chronic urinary retention unless renal function is impaired.

Gastrointestinal haemorrhage

98. B Oesophagoduodenoscopy
99. A Colonoscopy
100.A Colonoscopy

In the first case, any patient who attends the A&E Department with a massive fresh bleed per rectum which causes haemodynamic compromise should have an oesophagoduodenoscopy to exclude a bleeding peptic ulcer. Only after this has been excluded can one proceed with lower GI investigations.
In the second case, the elderly gentleman is not in shock and the nature of the bleeding is suggestive of a lower GI cause e.g. diverticular disease, colonic carcinoma. In this instance a colonoscopy would probably be the best first-line investigation.
In the third case, the young man who presents to the clinic with no local cause for his rectal bleeding should undergo a colonoscopy to exclude a polyp. This investigation is preferable to a barium enema as it may be therapeutic as well as diagnostic and has a higher specificity and sensitivity. The use of CT colonography for the screening of polyps and colonic cancer is presently undergoing evaluation.

END OF SYSTEM PAPER 4

1.   Epistaxis   Answers: C D

Epistaxis results from a wide range of local and systemic conditions. It may be a presenting feature of haematological disease e.g. leukaemia or lymphoma. The most common site of epistaxis is the anterior nasal septum (Little's area). If bleeding does not stop with pressure, then packing (anterior-nasal or post-nasal) is required. A Foley urinary catheter, not a Fogarty catheter is useful for staunching the haemorrhage. Sedation should be avoided as this may compromise respiration.

2.   Parotid gland tumours   Answers: A B D

80% of parotid tumours are benign and 80% of these are pleomorphic adenomas. 15% of salivary gland neoplasms are in the submandibular gland. A proportion of tumours are slow growing but should not be biopsied as they are at risk of tumour seeding along the tract. Otalgia (referred pain) may be a presenting feature.

3.   Submandibular gland   Answers: C D E

The submandibular gland consists of a deep and superficial part. The superficial part lies in the submandibular triangle, above and between the two bellies of digastric muscle. It is superficial to mylohyoid and hyoglossus. The lingual nerve lies first between the duct and the deep part of the gland, then crosses medially beneath the duct to ascend to the hyoglossus to supply the tongue. One-third of the gland lies below the lower border of the mandible and two-thirds above it.

4.   Enlarging thyroid gland   Answers: B E

The thyroid gland is invested in the pretracheal fascia, which is attached above to both the oblique line of the thyroid cartilage and body of the hyoid bone, laterally to the anterior surface of the carotid sheath underneath the sternocleidomastoid muscle, and below to the aortic arch. Thus, an enlarging thyroid gland cannot extend superiorly into the digastric triangle, but moves laterally over the internal jugular vein and substernally within the pretracheal fascia posterior to the left brachiocephalic vein, as the latter crosses the midline, displacing the vein downwards and anteriorly against the manubrium.

5.   Transection of sympathetic chain at root of neck   Answers: A B E

In Horner's syndrome, there is ptosis, pupillary constriction and occasional enophthalmos, and dryness and flushing of the skin of the head and neck. The sympathetic supply to the lungs is preserved as this originates below the lesion directly from the T1–4 ganglia of the sympathetic chain. Sympathetic fibres pass to the arm via grey rami from the middle and inferior cervical sympathetic ganglia through all roots of the brachial plexus.

6.   The middle meatus   Answer: B

The nasolacrimal duct drains into the inferior meatus; the sphenoidal air sinus into the sphenoethmoidal recess; and the posterior ethmoidal air sinus into the superior meatus. The middle meatus contains the bulla ethmoidalis of the middle ethmoidal air sinus which drains through a hiatus in the bulla. Olfactory epithelium containing the primary olfactory neurones lines the superior nasal recess (roof of the nasal cavity) undercover of the cribriform plate of the ethmoid bone.

7.   Familial hypercalcaemic hypocalciuria   Answer: A

Familial hypercalcaemic hypocalciuria is an autosomal dominant disease and may mimic primary hyperparathyroidism. Affected individuals are discovered because of asymptomatic hypercalcaemia. The primary defect is abnormal sensing of blood calcium by the parathyroid gland and renal tubule, causing inappropriate secretion of parathyroid hormone and excessive renal reabsorption.

8.   Le Fort III maxillary fracture   Answers: B D E

Fracture of the maxilla may occur at three levels: Le Fort I, II, and III. A Le Fort III fracture is the most severe and is the result of separation of the mid-facial skeleton from the anterior cranial base. Dental malocclusion is associated with displaced fractures. Le Fort II and III cause features of orbital and nasoethmoidal fractures. The characteristic clinical features of a Le Fort III are: panda eyes, gross mid-facial swelling, CSF rhinorrhoea, bilateral epistaxis and dental malocclusion. Only undisplaced fractures are treated conservatively.

9.   Right hemicolectomy   Answers: D E

When performing a right hemicolectomy, one encounters the gonadal vessels first and then the second part of the duodenum and right ureter. It is wise to clearly identify the ureter, though formal dissection and display is not always needed.

10.   Sigmoid volvulus   Answers: A E

Sigmoid volvulus is responsible for approximately 4% of all cases of intestinal obstruction in the UK. It is most common in the sixth and seventh decades, and in countries such as Africa. Predisposing factors include a redundant sigmoid colon and a short mesenteric attachment. Sigmoid volvulus is more common than caecal volvulus and is associated with a long history of disordered bowel habit with chronic constipation and laxative abuse. The bowel twists in an anticlockwise direction and gives rise to the appearance of an omega loop on AXR (convexity lying away from site of obstruction). Circulation is not impaired until one and a half twists have occurred.

11.   Faecal occult blood test   Answer: B

The amount of blood lost from the GI tract is normally between 0.5–1.5 ml/day. This amount is typically not detected by occult blood tests. Occult blood is commonly detected in the stool by FOB tests when there is no clinical evidence of bleeding or iron deficiency. Guaiac based FOB tests make use of the pseudoperoxidase activity of haemoglobin. Guaiac turns blue after oxidation. Guaiac based tests are generally best at detecting large distal lesions. Faecal rehydration markedly raises the sensitivity of the test but reduces its specificity. Whilst the dark green or black appearance of iron in the stool can be confused with the typical blue appearance of a positive guaiac based test, iron does not *per se* cause a positive reaction.

12.   Massive splenomegaly   Answers: B D E

Long-standing massive splenomegaly is known to be caused by chronic malaria, chronic myeloid leukaemia, myelofibrosis, kala-azar and schistosomiasis. Chagas' disease causes oesophageal and gastro-intestinal dilation. Hepatitis C is associated with cirrhosis of the liver which may in turn produce splenomegaly. However, the splenomegaly is only moderate.

13.   Glomus tumours   Answer: C

A glomus tumour is a benign tumour of blood vessels. It lies in the skin, two-thirds are found in the upper limb but they may also arise on the trunk. Half the glomus tumours develop in the digits and one-third subungally. Only 2% of glomus tumours are painless. Treatment is by surgical excision.

14.   Carotid artery stenosis   **Answers: B C E**

The initial investigation of choice for presumed carotid artery stenosis is duplex Doppler ultrasound. Further images may also be obtained by magnetic resonance angiography, arteriography either using contrast injection into the aortic arch or a selective injection into the common carotid artery or intravenous digital subtraction angiography. CT scan of the brain may be useful for confirming sites of previous strokes and excluding other intracranial causes of symptoms (e.g. AV malformation). This investigation is, however, not routine in some centres as the incidence of the conditions is low in the absence of any positive history or examination. Selective cannulation of the common carotid artery is associated with a higher incidence of embolic stroke and is very rarely used.

15.   The posterior tibial artery   **Answers: A C D E**

The popliteal artery divides into anterior and posterior tibial arteries, as it exits the popliteal fossa, anterior to the fibrous arch of the soleus muscle. The peroneal artery is the first branch of the posterior tibial artery. At the ankle joint, the posterior tibial artery passes deep to the flexor retinaculum.

16.   The portal vein   **Answers: B C E**

The portal vein is formed by the confluence of the superior mesenteric vein (lying to the right of the artery) and the splenic vein behind the neck of the pancreas. The terminals of the portal vein and the hepatic artery form, with the hepatic ductules, the triads of the liver in the corners of the hexagonal lobules. The central veins drain into the hepatic veins.

17.   Stenosis of the superficial femoral artery   **Answers: A B C D**

Superficial femoral artery stenosis is the commonest cause of intermittent claudication in the lower limbs. A stenosis may result in a fall in ankle pressure and can be rectified by a bypass or, if a short stenosis, by angioplasty.

18.   Portal vein thrombosis   **Answers: All true**

Portal vein thrombosis may occur secondarily to thrombophilia or septic thrombophlebitis, possibly in severe appendicitis. It is one of the causes of small bowel infarction. It may result in portal hypertension with small intestinal varices and splenomegaly.

19.   Compartment syndrome   Answer: D
Compartment syndrome results from an increased pressure within a closed compartment – thus with a Grade 3b open fracture where there is gross disruption of the soft tissues, a compartment syndrome is rare. The syndrome is associated with pain on stretching the muscles in the involved compartment (i.e. extension or dorsiflexion) and is diagnosed when the pressure is 30 mmHg – hence peripheral pulses are unaffected.

20.   Varicose veins   Answers: B C
Varicose veins are usually due to long saphenous vein incompetence and may cause leg ulcers or thrombophlebitis. Venous pressure falls on exercise, providing the deep veins are patent. Small varices can be obliterated with 5% ethanolamine; stronger solutions may cause skin ulceration.

21.   Complications of laparoscopic surgery   Answers: A C D E
Complications of laparoscopic surgery usually related to Verres needle insertion and insufflation i.e. abdominal wall emphysema, trocar injuries to bowel, bladder or major vessels. Diathermy or laser injuries usually occur off screen but may also be directly on screen. Pneumothorax and carbon dioxide embolus are the other well-known complications.

22.   Screening for colorectal carcinomas   Answers: A B D
Risk factors for colorectal carcinoma include ulcerative colitis, familial adenomatous polyposis and Gardner's syndrome. These patients should be screened on a regular basis. Peutz–Jeghers syndrome is an autosomal dominant condition characterised by circumoral mucocutaneous pigmentation associated with hamartomas in the small bowel. Hamartomas have been described in the stomach and colon. These polyps are multiple and present in childhood with bleeding, anaemia or small bowel obstruction.

23.   Crohn's disease   Answer: C
Crohn's disease runs a chronic relapsing course and cannot be cured by surgical excision. Bowel should be resected back to macroscopically normal intestine. When there are several, short segment small bowel strictures, multiple stricturoplasties are preferred to multiple small bowel resections, as the emphasis is on preservation of small bowel length. If proctocolectomy is indicated, an intersphincteric dissection should be performed to preserve perirectal tissues, and aid post-operative wound closure. Perianal abscesses, as at other times, require surgical drainage, but the surgery should be conservative. Antibiotics are helpful in controlling many of the anal manifestations of Crohn's disease.

24.   Colon cancer   Answers: B E

Colorectal cancer is the second commonest malignant cause of death in the UK after lung cancer. There is a marked male predominance for rectal cancer, and a slight female predominance for colonic cancer. The incidence is much less in Africa and Asia than in Western countries, perhaps reflecting diet and other environmental factors. There is an increasing relative incidence of right-sided to left-sided colonic carcinoma in Western countries.

25.   Inguinal region   Answers: A E

The pectineal ligament is otherwise known as Astley Cooper's ligament, the lacunar ligament as Gimbernat's ligament, and the inguinal ligament as Poupart's ligament. The transversalis fascia and Scarpa's fascia are not related structures. Cloquet's node lies within the femoral canal, and is said to drain the clitoris.

26.   Acute pancreatitis   Answers: D E

Early poor prognostic factors for acute pancreatitis include a blood glucose level of > 11 mmol/l in the absence of previously diagnosed diabetes, a serum calcium of < 2 mmol/l, a WCC $> 15 \times 10^9$/l, $pO_2 < 8$ kPa, a blood urea > 16 mmol/l despite adequate fluid replacement, serum albumin < 32 g/l, serum AST (SGOT) > 200 u/l, and serum LDH > 600 iu/l. These criteria are based on Ranson and Imrie systems. Haemoglobin and the degree of elevation of serum amylase are not predictors of outcome. C-reactive protein is also a good independent prognostic indicator.

27.   Acute cholecystitis   Answers: B C E

Ultrasound findings in acute cholecystitis include gall bladder calculi with posterior acoustic shadowing, biliary sludge, pericholecystic fluid, a thickened gall bladder wall (> 2–3 mm), and common bile duct dilatation (> 6 mm) in 10–15% of cases due to associated common bile duct calculi. The cystic duct itself is not well seen and is usually narrowed. Biliary sludge may also be seen in fasting patients and those who have been in ITU for several days.

28.   Femoral hernia   Answers: A B

Femoral hernias have a high risk of strangulation owing to the usually narrow femoral canal and hernial neck. The hernia itself is usually small and easily missed in the obese. They are more common in females. The neck of the sac lies below the level of the inguinal ligament, but if large, the hernial sac itself will extend anterior and above it. Scrotal skin invagination will reveal an empty inguinal canal.

29.   In gallstone disease
Answers: D E F

Most patients with gallstones are asymptomatic. The pain of biliary colic is due to gall bladder distension resulting from temporary cystic duct obstruction from a calculus impacted in Hartmann's pouch. Symptoms are relieved following spontaneous disimpaction. A mucocele is a gall bladder distended with mucus, which is not normally infected. An empyema is an intraluminal abscess whereby the gall bladder wall remains intact. Though it can lead to major sepsis, it is usually associated with lesser degrees of systemic disturbance. Acute cholecystitis infrequently progresses to perforation, but if it occurs it usually occurs at the fundus, or occasionally adjacent to an impacted stone.

30.   Solitary rectal ulcer syndrome
Answers: A B

Bright red rectal bleeding and excessive passage of mucus are present in > 90% of cases of solitary rectal ulcer syndrome. The condition itself is felt to be related to rectal trauma created by varied degrees of rectal prolapse. Histological features are those of smooth muscle fibres extending from a thickened muscularis mucosa into the lamina propria with associated fibrosis and mucosal ulceration. Pallisading basal cells is a feature of basal cell carcinoma. Solitary rectal ulcer syndrome has a very high recurrence rate following simple excision of visible rectal lesions. Solitary rectal ulcer syndrome is very difficult to treat, though biofeedback may be of benefit, or perhaps rectopexy in those who do not respond. Patients not infrequently come to stoma formation.

31.   Ulcerative colitis
Answers: B C D

Indications for surgery in ulcerative colitis include failure to respond to adequate medical treatment after five days, acute toxic megacolon with or without perforation, perforation, severe bleeding, failure of adequate medical treatment of chronic disease over a prolonged period of time, and the presence of confirmed dysplasia of any severity on colonic biopsies. Total colitis increases the long-term risk of developing colorectal carcinoma but is not an indication for surgery in itself.

32.   Duodenum
Answers: A C E

The third part of the duodenum lies posterior to the superior mesenteric vessels and uncinate process of the pancreas, and also overlies the aorta and beginning of the inferior mesenteric artery. The root of the small bowel mesentery is attached near its termination on the left. The second part of the duodenum overlies the right ureter and renal vessels in the hilum of the right kidney, separated from the renal artery by the vein.

33.   The kidneys   Answers: B E

The kidneys first develop in the pelvis and ascend to eventually lie with hila in the transpyloric plane. Only their inferior poles are palpable in the lumbar region. The right kidney is not covered by the head of the pancreas but overlies the renal vessels at the hilum in the concavity of the duodenum. The tail of the pancreas covers the hilum and lower aspect of the upper pole of the left kidney. The upper poles of both kidneys lie on the lateral arcuate ligaments of the diaphragm.

34.   Superficial inguinal lymph nodes   Answers: A B C E

The superficial inguinal lymph nodes comprise a proximal group, below the inguinal ligament, and a distal group, lying alongside the termination of the great saphenous vein. The lateral nodes of the former group drain the buttock and back, and also the flank below the waist. The medial nodes drain the anterior abdominal wall below the umbilicus including the external genitalia (excluding the testis), lower anal canal, and perineum. The fundus of the uterus drains via lymphatics accompanying the round ligament. The distal group of nodes drain superficial lymphatics from the lower limb.

35.   Inguinal canal   Answers: B C D E

The inferior epigastric artery lies medial to the deep ring. The lacunar ligament forms the medial part of the floor of the inguinal canal, and the medial wall of the femoral canal. The transversalis fascia forms the posterior wall of the inguinal canal throughout, strengthened by the conjoint tendon medially. The roof is formed by the arching fibres of both the transversus abdominis and internal oblique muscles. The canal transmits the ilioinguinal nerve which enters from the side, through the superficial inguinal ring.

36.   The obturator nerve   Answers: A B E

The obturator nerve arises from the anterior division of the ventral L2–4 rami. After passing through the obturator foramen, cutaneous branches are given off from the anterior division of the nerve. A branch of the posterior division supplies the knee joint. None of the peripheral nerves in the body contain parasympathetic axons.

37.   Osteosarcoma   Answers: B E

Osteochondromas that increase in size after skeletal maturity may have undergone malignant change but the tumour is usually a chondrosarcoma. Osteosarcomas affect the metaphyses – Ewing's sarcoma tends to affect the diaphyses. Most tumours can be resected and treated with adjuvant chemotherapy.

38. Suppurative tenosynovitis

Answers: C D E

Kanavel's cardinal signs of suppurative tenosynovitis of the flexor tendons are: fingers held in slight flexion; pain on passive movement; fusiform swelling and tenderness along the flexor sheath extending into the palm. The patient is not usually systemically unwell.

39. Deep laceration to the thenar eminence

Answers: B E

The superficial palmar arch is incomplete over the thenar eminence. The radial artery passes over the dorsum of the wrist. The flexor digitorum superficialis tendons lie in the carpal tunnel medial to the median nerve and thenar eminence. All these structures therefore escape damage from the above laceration. However, the recurrent branch of the median nerve and the adductor pollicis muscle would be involved, and thus movements of the thumb would be restricted.

40. Fracture of the ulna

Answer: B

The head of the radius articulates with the lateral two carpal bones and it is thus the radius and not the ulna which usually fractures after falls on the outstretched hand. Since the ulna does not articulate at the wrist, there is no wrist involvement and accordingly movement at the wrist, including adduction is unimpaired. Similarly, movements of the little finger, mediated by the superficial and deep flexors and extensors, are unaffected since the lower end of the ulna does not give attachment to these muscles. Pronation is, however, impaired because of pain either resulting from involvement of the inferior radio-ulnar joint, or movement of the fracture site across the attachment of the pronator quadratus muscle.

41. The ankle joint

Answer: C

The lateral malleolus is grooved by the peroneus brevis tendon; the medial malleolus by the tibialis posterior tendon. The superficial part of the deltoid ligament is attached to the sustentaculum tali. Posterior to the medial malleolus, the tibial nerve lies posterior to the posterior tibial artery; the two lying between the flexor hallucis longus tendons posteriorly, and the flexor digitorum longus tendons anteriorly.

42. Supracondylar fracture in a child

Answers: A D E

Brachial artery spasm with or without actual intimal damage is a feared complication. Compartment syndrome may occur with or without arterial damage. Malunion of this fracture is relatively common but it is usually a cubitus varus (not valgus) deformity. Injury to any of the major nerves may occur but depending which series is believed, damage to the anterior interosseus branch of the median nerve is the most frequent. Supracondylar fractures by definition occur proximal to the growth plate so no growth arrest should occur.

43.   Congenital diaphragmatic hernia   Answers: A B C D

Diaphragmatic hernia usually occurs due to failure of closure of the pleuroperitoneal canal (8th week). It is associated with hypoplasia of the lungs and may present with respiratory distress at birth. 85% of congenital diaphragmatic hernias are left-sided and over 50% are associated with congenital defects. Surgical correction is delayed until the infant is stable. Infants may require inotropic support and pulmonary vasodilators (e.g. nitric oxide) or extra-corporeal membrane oxygenation. Late presentations include vomiting and a failure to thrive.

44.   Meckel's diverticulum   Answers: A B C D

A Meckel's diverticulum is found in approximately 2% of the population. It can produce a wide range of complications the most common being obstruction. Others include rectal bleeding and inflammation. It may contain ectopic gastric mucosa or pancreatic tissue. The gastric mucosa in the Meckel's can be localised by a technetium scan (^{99m}Tc).

45.   Duodenal atresia   Answer: A

Duodenal atresia is more frequent in children with Down's syndrome (Trisomy 21). Surgery to correct duodenal atresia usually involves a duodenostomy which may be delayed for three or four days after birth. The typical X-ray appearance of a double bubble is usually quite obvious when the child is a few hours old.

46.   Infantile hypertrophic pyloric stenosis   Answer: A

Infantile hypertrophic pyloric stenosis is a very common condition occurring in 3–5:1000 live births. The vomiting is typically effortless and forceful (projectile) and is not bile stained as the intestinal obstruction is proximal to the ampulla of Vater. There is a well-recognised familial association. Babies born prematurely may develop pyloric stenosis. Although a test feed is helpful in palpation of the pyloric olive, it is equally possible to feel it whilst the infant is asleep, or at rest quietly sucking on a dummy.

47.   Intussusception   Answers: A D E
Intussusception, is the commonest cause of small bowel obstruction in a child under the age of eighteen months. The classical presentation is of colicky abdominal pain associated with 'red currant jelly' stool rather than the 'brick red' coloured stool. The latter is more typical of a bleeding Meckel's diverticulum. A lead point occurs in over 25% of children presenting over the age of eighteen months with an intussusception. A pathological lead point is less common under this age. Approximately 75% of children with an intussusception can be treated effectively with an air enema in which oxygen is gently pumped into an infant's rectum to 'blow' the intussusception back. An air enema should not be attempted in a child with peritonitis or continuing signs of shock despite appropriate resuscitation.

48.   Organ-confined prostate cancer   Answers: A C E
The complete incontinence rate following radical prostatectomy is 2–5%. Cryotherapy is not a widely accepted treatment option for localised disease. Its use is mainly described in the treatment of salvage situations. Brachytherapy implies the implantation of radioactive iodine or palladium seeds within the prostate.

49.   Carcinoma of the penis   Answers: A B C
Carcinoma of the penis is rare in males circumcised at birth. Circumcision in under-developed countries is far less common. The cure rates for surgery, external beam radiotherapy or brachytherapy are similar although local recurrence is not uncommon when organ preservation is attempted. Bouin's medium is used to store sperm retrieved during scrotal exploration for infertility. Bowen's disease (carcinoma in-situ, also known as erythroplasia de Queyrat when exclusively on glans) is a premalignant condition. 50% of palpable inguinal lymph nodes at presentation are due to inflammation or infection, and a six week course of antibiotics is advised following which the nodes are reassessed.

50. Neuropathic bladder dysfunction   Answers: All true

The causes of neuropathic bladder dysfunction can be divided into cerebral lesions (e.g. CVA, dementia, Parkinsonism), spinal lesions (e.g. trauma, multiple sclerosis, spina bifida) and peripheral nerve lesions (e.g. following pelvic surgery or diabetes mellitus). Lesions of the sacral cord or peripheral nerves cause an underactive detrusor and urethra. Lesions of the supra-spinal cord cause loss of inhibitory impulses so causing detrusor overreactivity and unco-ordinated activity of detrusor and urethra. Lesions above the pons cause loss of cerebral inhibiton and may produce overactive detrusor. Detrusor and urethral activity remain unco-ordinated.

51. Urinary incontinence   Answers: A C D E

Following TURP the causes of incontinence are usually a UTI or detrusor instability. Damage to the external sphincter is rare. TVT (trans-vaginal-tape) is sited around the mid-urethra. A pelvic floor contraction may inhibit an involuntary detrusor contraction as well as strengthen the pelvic floor in stress incontinence.

52. Stone in ureter   Answers: A B C

A 4 mm stone in the distal ureter is likely to pass spontaneously. If conservative management fails, ESWL or ureteroscopy is advised. Ureteric stenting is an option in an obstructed system and may be performed at the time of ureteroscopy. HIFU has been described in the treatment of some tissue tumours but has insufficient energy to fragment calculi. Oral fluids should be encouraged after the patient is stone-free to prevent recurrence.

Medical therapy for surgical conditions

61.	Azathioprine	C	Resistant Crohn's disease
62.	Anastrozole	E	Breast cancer
63.	Mithramycin	A	Hypercalcaemia
64.	Carbimazole	F	Thyrotoxicosis
65.	Flutamide	D	Disseminated prostatic cancer
66.	Streptozotocin	B	Carcinoid syndrome

Azathioprine may control Crohn's disease resistant to steroids, and may allow steroid-sparing in individual patients. It needs to be administered at least for 2–3 months to assess clinical effect. Anastrozole, an aromatase inhibitor, is now a second-line treatment of breast cancer after tamoxifen. Mithramycin is a cytotoxic antibiotic which prevents osteoclast function and rapidly reduces serum calcium in cases of malignant hypercalcaemia from bony metastatases. Flutamide is a non-steroidal pure androgen agonist. Streptozotocin in an effective cytotoxic chemotherapeutic agent used in carcinoid syndrome.

Hernias

67.	Dual sacs straddling the inferior epigastric vessels	E	Pantaloon hernia
68.	Two separate loops of bowel	C	Maydl's hernia
69.	The posterior wall of the hernial sac is formed by a herniating viscus	D	Sliding hernia
70.	Portion of circumference of the bowel	A	Richter's hernia
71.	Meckel's diverticulum	B	Littre's hernia

In a sliding hernia the posterior wall of the hernial sac is formed by a herniating viscus. This is usually sigmoid colon or bladder. Particular care is required during repair not to injure the herniated viscus.

Jaundice

72.	Chlorpromazine induced jaundice	B	Hepatic jaundice
73.	Chronic active hepatitis	B	Hepatic jaundice
74.	Halothane induced jaundice	B	Hepatic jaundice
75.	Thalassaemia	A	Pre-hepatic jaundice
76.	Sclerosing cholangitis	C	Post-hepatic jaundice
77.	Hepatic abscesses	B	Hepatic jaundice
78.	Rotor's syndrome	A	Pre-hepatic jaundice

Pre-hepatic causes of jaundice include the haemolytic anaemias and the familial non-haemolytic hyperbilirubinaemias such as Gilbert's and Rotor's syndromes. Hepatic causes include acute viral or drug-induced (halothane, chlorpromazine) hepatitis, other hepatoxic substances (alcohol, carbon tetrachloride), cirrhosis, chronic active hepatitis, hepatic tumours, hydatid disease, and liver abscesses. Post-hepatic causes include porta hepatis lymph nodes, sclerosing cholangitis, biliary atresia, bile duct carcinoma, pancreatic carcinoma and choledocholithiasis.

Infective and non-infective intestinal inflammation

79. Is associated with an acute   B   Yersinia enterocolitis
    ileitis and inflamed mesenteric
    lymph nodes
80. The main histological features are   D   Infective colitis
    oedema of the lamina propria and a
    predominantly polymorphonuclear
    infiltrate
81. Is postulated to be due to a local   E   Diversion colitis
    butyrate deficiency
82. Is typically associated with   A   Amoebic dysentery
    flask-shaped ulcers
83. Is associated with characteristic   C   Pseudomonas colitis
    yellow plaques on sigmoidoscopy

Amoebic dysentery is typically associated with flask-shaped ulcers in the large bowel, caused by *E. histolytica*. The ulcers have overhanging edges and a longitudinal axis at right angles to the colon. Yersinia enterocolitis is associated with an acute ileitis with inflamed mesenteric lymph nodes. The terminal ileum and caecum are inflamed and oedematous, with superficial mucosal ulceration. Pseudomembranous colitis is associated with characteristic yellow plaques on sigmoidoscopy. Infective colitis gives rise to features of oedema of the lamina propria and a predominant polymorphonuclear infiltrate. This helps differentiation from other forms of colitis such as Crohn's disease or ulcerative colitis, which have both chronic and acute cells. Diversion colitis is thought to be due to a local butyrate deficiency, and may be treated with short chain fatty acid solutions.

Paediatric investigations

84. A 10-hour-old term female with persistent non-bile stained vomiting	A	A 'Double Bubble' on plain AXR
85. A 10-day-old baby, born at 31 weeks, with bile stained vomiting and bleeding per rectum	D	Intra-mural gas on plain AXR
86. An 8-month-old infant with colicky abdominal pain and bleeding PRF	A	'Target' lesion on abdominal ultrasound
87. A 2-day-old baby with abdominal distension, bile stained vomiting and failure to pass meconium	B	A 'cone' on contrast enema

Dilatation of the renal pelvis without dilatation of the corresponding ureter might be due to pelviureteric junction obstruction (PUJ). Diuretic renography may distinguish an obstructed system from that of a dilated but normally draining system. Persistent non-bile stained vomiting in a newborn infant may indicate a diagnosis of duodenal atresia. The typical radiological feature is the double bubble seen on plain AXR (an air filled dilated stomach and first part of duodenum creating two discrete air shadows). A premature baby presenting with bile stained vomiting and rectal bleeding is at high risk of suffering from necrotizing enterocolitis. The typical radiological feature of this condition is gas within the bowel wall on plain AXR. It may be associated with gas in the portal system and/or free air in the abdomen when the disease progresses to intestinal perforation.

An eight-month-old infant with colicky abdominal pain and rectal bleeding is likely to have intussusception which may be diagnosed on abdominal ultrasound by the presence of a 'target lesion' or by Gastrografin enema. The 'target' lesion represents the layers of the bowel, one invaginated inside the other seen in transverse section.

Hirschsprung's disease typically presents in the first few days of life with abdominal distension, bile stained vomiting and failure to pass meconium. On contrast enema, the diagnosis can easily be made by the presence of a cone between collapsed distal bowel (usually rectum or sigmoid) and proximal dilated bowel. The cone represents the approximate area of the transition between normally ganglionated bowel and distal aganglionic bowel.

Hypochloraemic metabolic alkalosis is typical of pyloric stenosis, air filled cysts in the left chest will be typical of a diaphragmatic hernia although differential diagnosis includes congenital cystic disease of the lung, clubbed renal calyces noted on micturating cystography will be associated with more severe vesicoureteric reflux.

Peripheral nerve anatomy

88. E   Common peroneal
89. C   Obturator
90. A   Saphenous   — ▷
91. G   Sciatic

The most common neural injury in the lower limb is to the common peroneal nerve, either by direct trauma, or pressure from a plaster cast at the neck of the fibula. Common presentations are 'foot drop' (paralysis of the extensor muscles supplied by the deep peroneal branch), and inversion of the foot (less obvious because there is paralysis of peroneus longus and brevis muscles – superficial peroneal nerve and the tibialis anterior muscle is also paralysed – deep peroneal nerve).

Thus, only the inverting action of tibialis posterior is present. Anaesthesia over the lower lateral calf and dorsum of the foot also develops (superficial peroneal nerve). Note that the lateral cutaneous nerve of the calf branches arises from the common peroneal nerve above the lesion in the popliteal fossa and, accordingly, sensation over the upper lateral skin of the calf is normal.

Pelvic pathology may present with referred pain over the cutaneous distribution of the obturator nerve because the inflamed lateral pelvic peritoneum is supplied by the nerve as it passes retroperitoneally through the pelvis. In this case, the ovarian tumour growing out from the posterior surface of the broad ligament into the rectouterine pouch, is irritating the peritoneum of the lateral pelvic wall.

L5/S1 disc prolapse damages the S1 spinal nerve. The L5 spinal nerve escapes injury because it exits the spinal canal above the prolapse in the L5 intervertebral canal. The S1 dermatome (supplied by the sural nerve) is found over the lower lateral part of the calf and lateral aspect of the foot.

In 20% of fracture dislocations of the hip, the sciatic nerve may be injured as it passes over the posterior aspect of the joint capsule. All flexors and extensors below the knee are paralysed and all skin is anaesthetic except for those areas innervated by the saphenous (medial calf and medial foot), and posterior cutaneous nerve of the thigh (upper posterior aspect of the calf). Paralysis of the hamstring muscles also occurs, but is difficult to assess clinically because of the extent of the trauma over the buttock in these cases.

Anatomy of the posterior abdominal wall

92.	Tracts pus to the femoral triangle	B	Psoas major muscle
93.	Lies in the root of the sigmoid mesentery	D	Ureter
94.	Lies behind the aorta	E	Sympathetic trunk
95.	Lies behind the kidney	F	Ilioinguinal nerve
96.	Lies medial to the left ureter	H	Superior rectal artery
97.	Is embedded in the psoas major muscle	C	Lumbar plexus
98.	Lies anterior to the subcostal vessels	A	Kidney
99.	Contacts the right suprarenal gland	G	Bare area of liver

- A psoas abscess tracts within the tough psoas fascia to point below the inguinal ligament in the femoral triangle.
- The left ureter crosses the pelvic brim over the sacroiliac joint in front of the divisions of the common iliac vessels within the apex of the 'V' shaped root of the sigmoid mesentery.
- The left sympathetic trunk lies behind the left margin of the aorta.
- The ilioinguinal nerve lies behind the kidney on each side.
- The superior rectal artery (a branch of the inferior mesenteric artery) lies medial to the left ureter throughout its course.
- The lumbar plexus is embedded in the psoas major muscle.
- The kidney lies anterior to the subcostal vessels and nerve on each side.
- The bare area of the liver contacts the right suprarenal gland.

Testicular tumours

100.D Radiotherapy
101.D Radiotherapy
102.G Retroperitoneal lymph node dissection

The present treatment of stage I seminoma is radical orchidectomy and prophylactic radiotherapy to the retroperitoneal nodes, although trials are underway comparing adjuvant radiotherapy with carboplatin (adjuvant chemotherapy). Intra-tubular germ cell neoplasia inevitably develops into cancer, therefore a prophylactic dose of 20 Gy radiotherapy is given to the remaining testis after sperm banking has been offered. The treatment of residual nodes following chemotherapy and normalisation of tumour markers is retro-peritoneal lymph node dissection.

ANSWERS – Systems Paper 5

MRCS SYSTEM INDEX

PASTEST REVISION COURSES FOR MRCS

Feeling in need of a helping hand towards success in your exams?

PasTest has over twenty-five years' experience in helping doctors to pass first time, with specially tailored courses to make the most of your valuable revision time.

Over 4000 candidates attend our courses each year at locations throughout the UK. To give you the most up-to-date information and help you to achieve the best results, we constantly update and improve our courses based on feedback from those who attend.

Our course material is continually updated to ensure the best possible revision for the exam. You will receive hundreds of exam-type MCQs and EMQs, with explanations and detailed handouts, and mock exam practice.

- **Two-day MCQ/EMQ Courses**
Intensive revision in either Core Modules or Systems Modules. An opportunity to study over the weekend – ideal if you are unable to take study leave.

- **Three-day MCQ/EMQ Courses**
Following feedback from previous MRCS candidates, we have extended the two-day course to include extra teaching time for the more complex areas.

- **Clinical and Viva Courses**
Run in association with various hospitals, our two-day clinical and viva courses offer small teaching groups to provide you with the best help possible.

HAVE YOU APPLIED FOR FREE PASTEST MEMBERSHIP?

PasTest Membership benefits include access to an exclusive members' area on the PasTest website where you can download free exam material, special members' discounts on courses and books and the most up-to-date revision material throughout your postgraduate study.

For queries on books, courses or benefits of the PasTest Membership scheme, please call our dedicated Customer Services team on **0800 980 9814**. Alternatively, visit our website at **www.pastest.co.uk**.

MRCS Core Modules: Essential Revision Notes   1 901198 36 7
Ed. J Elkabir & A Khadra

MRCS System Modules: Essential Revision Notes   1 901198 41 3
Ed. C Parchment Smith & C Hernon

These new books give a unique presentation of the key elements of all subjects covered in the Core and System Modules syllabus. Unlike conventional textbooks, the essential facts in each subject are presented in note form with special attention given to areas which are often poorly understood. Designed to make learning easier, no candidate should be without these excellent books.

- The definitive guides to revision for the MRCS examination
- Vital facts presented in user-friendly format
- All areas of the syllabus covered in concise note form
- Diagrams, lists, illustrations and bullet points to aid learning
- Essential information highlighted throughout each chapter

MRCS Core Modules: MCQs and EMQs   1 901198 09 X
A Williams, C Chan, T Hennigan & L Barker

MRCS System Modules: MCQs and EMQs   1 901198 10 3
A Williams, C Chan, T Hennigan & L Barker

These two books have been devised to comprehensively cover all aspects of the Core and System Modules necessary for the exam. Extensive explanations are provided for each question and are presented in an easily accessible format.

- Over 300 new MCQs and EMQs covering each of the Modules in its own section
- Correct answers help to identify weak areas of knowledge in time for further study
- Similar in content and level of difficulty to current exam questions
- Expert advice on successful examination technique

PASTEST REVISION BOOKS

MRCS Core Modules: Practice Papers   **1 901198 45 6**
C Chan

MRCS System Modules: Practice Papers   **1 901198 46 4**
C Chan

Compiled by a team of experienced surgeons, these new books feature five Practice Papers, providing an excellent framework for study and revision for those preparing for the written component of the MRCS exam.

- Five new Practice Papers
- Answers and detailed teaching notes for each question
- Similar in content and level of difficulty to current exam questions
- Expert advice on successful examination technique

To order any of the above titles, please contact PasTest on Freephone:

0800 980 9814

PasTest, FREEPOST, Knutsford, Cheshire, WA16 7BR
Fax: 01565 650264 E-mail: books@pastest.co.uk
or order on-line at www.pastest.co.uk

PASTEST
Dedicated to your success